*Leah Brooks*

# BAKING with KIDS

## MAKE BREADS, MUFFINS, COOKIES, PIES, PIZZA DOUGH, AND MORE!

Photography by Scott Peterson

**Quarry Books**
100 Cummings Center, Suite 406L
Beverly, MA 01915

quarrybooks.com • quarryspoon.com

© 2015 by Quarry Books

Photography © 2015 Scott Peterson

First published in the United States of America in 2015 by

Quarry Books, a member of
Quarto Publishing Group USA Inc.
100 Cummings Center, Suite 406-L
Beverly, Massachusetts 01915-6101
Telephone: (978) 282-9590
Fax: (978) 283-2742
www.quarrybooks.com

Visit www.QuarrySPOON.com and help us celebrate
food and culture one spoonful at a time!

10 9 8 7 6 5 4 3 2 1

ISBN: 978-1-59253-977-2

Digital edition published in 2015

eISBN: 978-1-62788-158-6

**Library of Congress Cataloging-in-Publication Data**

Brooks, Leah.
  Baking with kids : make breads, muffins, cookies, pies,
pizza dough, and more! / Leah Brooks ; photography by
Scott Peterson.
    pages cm — (Hands-on family)
  ISBN 978-1-59253-977-2 (paperback)
  1.  Baking. 2.  Family recreation.  I. Title.
  TX765.B82956 2015
  641.81'5--dc23

                                    2014025588

Book Design: Laura H. Couallier, Laura Herrmann Design

Photography: Scott Peterson Productions, Inc.

Shutterstock.com: page 28

Printed in China

This book is dedicated to Holly,
for teaching me how to cook from the heart
and helping me realize my dreams.

# CONTENTS

HANDS-ON FAMILY

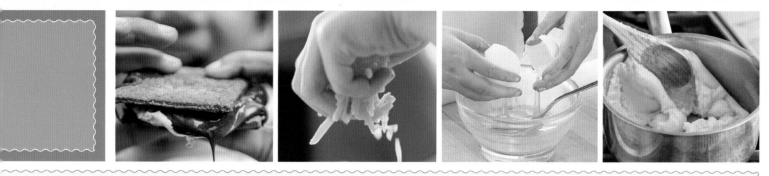

# INTRODUCTION

I've always been happiest in the kitchen. In my early teens, there were quite a few afternoons when I came home feeling defeated after a rough day at school. It was a simpler time, when having a bad haircut or dealing with braces seemed like an insurmountable obstacle to hurdle. I found solace within the walls of my kitchen, in the basic task of making chocolate chip cookies.

I made the same recipe so many times that eventually I knew it by heart. I found the process of measuring, mixing, and baking to be wonderfully repetitive and soothing. It was therapeutic to know that if I just followed the steps, I would get a consistent batch of delicious, warm cookies. You might call it "kitchen therapy."

I not only loved feeding myself this treat, but I also found even more pleasure in sharing those cookies with my family. I recall my mom telling her friends that I made *the best* chocolate chip cookies. It made me proud and gave me confidence. While good grades in school also made my parents proud—which certainly boosted my confidence—the baking was a personal source of pride that helped me unwind from those stressful days at school.

At the after-school cooking program where I teach children how to cook, it is my goal to help my students find their own version of kitchen therapy. I don't often see children come into my kitchen visibly upset or gloomy, but on those rare occasions it's wonderful to see their mood change as they immerse themselves in a recipe, and then smile when they see their finished product come out of the oven.

I hope that this book provides you and your family with the tools needed to create your own kind of kitchen therapy. Baking at home may seem time-consuming, but it functions as a fun activity that also provides wholesome alternatives to store-bought snacks. In this book you'll find tips on how to include your child and make baking at home work with your family's busy schedule. Although it may seem daunting at first, the smell of fresh-baked goods wafting throughout your home will be worth the effort.

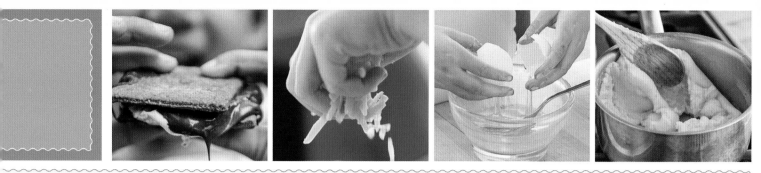

# HOW TO USE THIS BOOK

**I am always so impressed and surprised by how capable children are in the kitchen. Young children often default to wanting the adult to help or do a kitchen task for them. Although parents are used to caring for and doing things for their children, I suggest urging them to try even the most challenging steps on their own at first. When children realize that they are indeed capable, they gain independence that ultimately boosts their confidence.**

In this book, you'll find helpful tips for including young children (ages 5 to 7) in the sections called "For smaller hands." These are the techniques that I use when cooking with kids in my school to help remove obstacles and make otherwise difficult tasks seem less daunting. There are some tasks you would expect to be challenging for kids, where, instead of simply completing the task for them, you can suggest a different approach that will make the concept easier to grasp, and ultimately master. Before long they'll be showing you how it's done!

In each recipe, you'll find a list of ingredients and tools needed. Gathering all of your ingredients and tools before you begin making a recipe will help you get organized and be prepared for all the steps. There is a French phrase for this method, *misé en place*, which means "everything in its place." If you do not have an ingredient, there may be alternatives available. When a less common ingredient is called for, the recipe will list alternatives when possible. But sometimes the less-common ingredient is important and cannot be omitted or substituted. Leaveners are an example of one of these key ingredients that cannot be substituted, because leaveners are crucial to the recipe's success. Various types of flour called for in a recipe are examples of some common ingredients that can be substituted. White whole wheat flour, for instance, can be replaced with all-purpose flour without any negative effects. I welcome you to try new things, and have fun in the kitchen!

One important thing to remember when you are cooking with kids is that mistakes do happen. This doesn't mean that you should assume that things won't always work out when involving your kids in the kitchen; it simply means that you should try to keep an open mind about the end result. It might not be perfect in your eyes, but your kids will likely be proud of the result just the same.

I hope that you have as much fun making these recipes with your kids as I do making them with my students, friends, and family! Happy baking!

# Chapter 1

# KIDS' KITCHEN SAFETY: *Respecting the Kitchen*

*Always wash your hands before cooking!*

The kitchen is a fun place to be, but it is important to teach children to listen carefully and be respectful while working in the kitchen. There are many potentially dangerous situations that can arise if proper safety rules are not established and followed closely. Before you start baking with your child, please read this chapter through from beginning to end.

## KITCHEN RULES

Here are a few of the basic kitchen rules that I establish at the beginning of all the classes I teach. I suggest you come up with a phrase or signal for when you would like to get your child's attention. A common phrase teachers use is "1-2-3 eyes on me," and the children respond with "1-2 eyes on you." Feel free to add other rules for your family as needed.

# KNIFE SAFETY

Remember that no matter what their age, all children have different attention spans and motor skills. Use your judgment when giving children knives. Some older children may not be ready for a serrated knife. Have all children start with butter knives. Explain that even though butter knives are not sharp, the children need to demonstrate that they know the proper way to handle the knife before moving on to serrated knives. When children demonstrate that they can use a knife safely, you can decide whether they are ready to advance to a sharper knife. Think of learning to use a knife as a system similar to the colored belt system in karate, in that you must achieve certain skills and practice in order to advance.

- Small children (ages 4 to 6) use butter knives and bench scrapers (see tools on pages 17 and 18) to chop.

- Children ages 7 to 9 can use small serrated knifes or paring knives.

- Children ages 10 to 12 can use small chef's knives. Larger chef's knives are harder to handle.

- Even children age 12 should learn how to use smaller knives before moving up to a chef's knife.

- What to look out for: Overly confident children are prone to accidents. Slow down when chopping. Learn how to chop precisely and you will naturally get faster at it.

- No ninja chef chopping!

*Smaller chef's knives are easier for older children to use.*

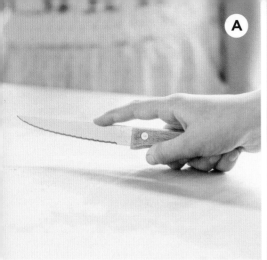

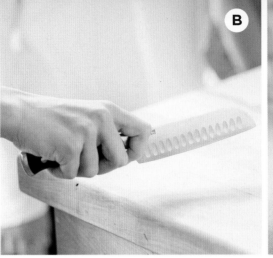

*To hold a serrated paring knife, place your index finger on top for stability.*

*To hold a chef's knife, pinch the blade with your index finger and thumb.*

*The bridge slicing technique.*

## How to Teach a Child to Use a Knife

1 *How to hold a knife.* Before even picking up the knife, notice which side is sharp and which side is dull. This might seem like a silly thing to do, but it helps children become more aware of the tools they are using and the danger of not paying attention. Use your dominant hand to hold the knife.

- For paring and butter knives, grip the handle of the knife and place your index finger top of the knife (the dull side). Having your finger on top gives you better control over the knife. (A)

- For larger chef's knives, grip the handle of the knife close to the blade. Place your index finger and your thumb on either side of the base of the blade and pinch it. Holding the knife this way makes the knife almost an extension of your hand, giving you more control over it. (B)

2 *How to hold what you are cutting.* Safely holding the food you are cutting is just as, if not more, important than proper knife handling. When chopping, use one hand to hold the knife and the other to hold the food. Always cut on top of a stable cutting board. To prevent your cutting board from slipping, place a damp towel or folded damp paper towel under the cutting board. Children should never hold food items above the cutting board and attempt to chop.

Notice the stability of what you are cutting. Is it round? Does it have a flat surface? Does it move around when placed on a flat surface? Before chopping, create a flat surface on the food.

- Use the bridge technique: Hold the food item with your thumb on one side and the rest of your fingers on top, creating a bridge. Use your knife to cut partway down the middle. Then, slice down and cut it completely. Now turn the item to rest on the flat surface you just created and continue cutting. (C)

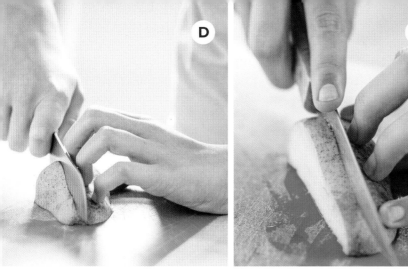

Use the bear claw technique to protect your fingers while cutting foods.

Slice back and forth; do not apply force!

## USING SHARP TOOLS

### Graters

Graters are sharp tools and have the potential to cut fingers. To avoid accidents, children should grate slowly and carefully. Once pieces become too small, have children pass off grating to adults.

### Peelers

Peelers are also sharp tools and need to be used with caution. Always peel food items on a work surface for stability. When peeling, peel away from hands to avoid cuts.

- Next, use the "bear claw" technique: Grip your food with your fingers tightly tucked under your knuckles, like a bear claw. This protects your fingers when you are chopping and helps guide the size of your cuts. (D)

3 *Let the knife do the work for you.* Never push down using excessive pressure on a knife. This means that your knife is too dull to cut whatever is on your cutting board and the knife may go to one side or the other, potentially into your hand. Cut in a slicing motion. With this technique, a sharp knife is a safer knife, because you do not have to use too much force. That being said, I do not recommend giving sharp knives to young children. Make sure that they master the butter knife and work their way up to sharp knives. Children start on serrated knives after using butter knives because it enforces the slicing motion. (E)

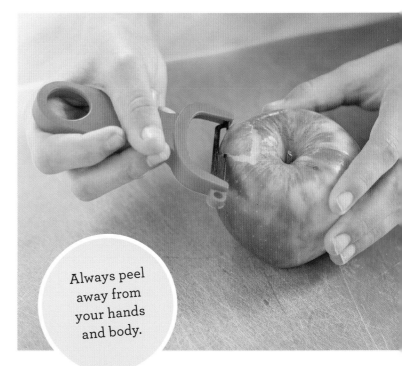

Always peel away from your hands and body.

*When accompanied by an adult, children can stand on a sturdy stool and assist at the stove.*

# USING THE OVEN

Before removing hot pans from the oven, make sure you've done the following:

- Confirm that small children are a safe distance away. Explain that you will be taking something very hot out of the oven and even though they might be excited to see it, it's not safe to be too close when adults are removing hot things from the oven.

- Find a spot in the kitchen that is out of reach of children for cooling ingredients on hot pans. In culinary school, an instructor once told me to assume every pan is hot. Tell children not to reach for a cookie on a cookie sheet, but to wait until it is on a plate or in a cookie jar. Make it a rule never to touch a cookie sheet if it is on the counter or table, explaining that these pans could be very hot and can easily cause burns if touched.

# USING THE STOVE

Most stove tops are a bit high for children to reach. Find a sturdy stool so your child can stand next to you when working at the stove. During my classes, I have children use the stove to cook ingredients that are cooked at a low heat *and* don't have a huge risk of sputtering. Make sure the stirring utensil is long so that the child is farther away from the edge of the pot or pan. Ensure that all pot and pan handles are pointed to the right or left, not sticking straight out from the stove. It is easy to bump into a handle sticking straight out, causing hot contents to spill!

*Place finished baked goods on a plate when cool.*

*Have your child help with the dishes!*

# CLEAN AS YOU GO

Because you may be using sharp tools or handling hot pans, the clean-as-you-go rule is very important. Spilling flour on the ground creates a slippery surface, which is dangerous and should be cleaned up immediately. The same rule applies for liquid spills.

Have your children help with the cleanup. It's fun to make and eat tasty treats, but a messy kitchen is not fun if you have to clean it up by yourself. Take a break between steps to see whether there is anything to do to help clean up. Are you done with that measuring spoon? Can you wash and reuse a utensil for a recipe?

When I'm teaching kids to cook, I rely on bubbles to help make cleaning fun for small children. Prepare a small amount of dish soap and warm water in a bowl with a sponge. Show your child how to squeeze excess water from the sponge before using it to clean a countertop. Bubbles are enticing and exciting, and they let you and the children visibly see what you have already cleaned! When children are finished scrubbing, use a clean, damp cloth to wipe the surface clean. Learning these skills early on will help them (and you) keep the kitchen clean even when there's a little person with a big cooking project.

*Scrubbing the work surface with soapy bubbles makes the task more fun.*

15

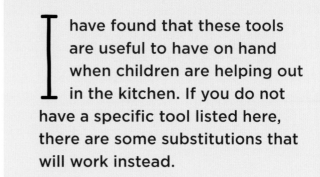

I have found that these tools are useful to have on hand when children are helping out in the kitchen. If you do not have a specific tool listed here, there are some substitutions that will work instead.

## HELPFUL KITCHEN TOOLS

### Baking Sheets

I use rimmed baking sheets for all the recipes in this book. The rim catches any liquids like butter or fruit juices that may leak out of baked goods and drip onto the bottom of the oven. This is especially useful for recipes

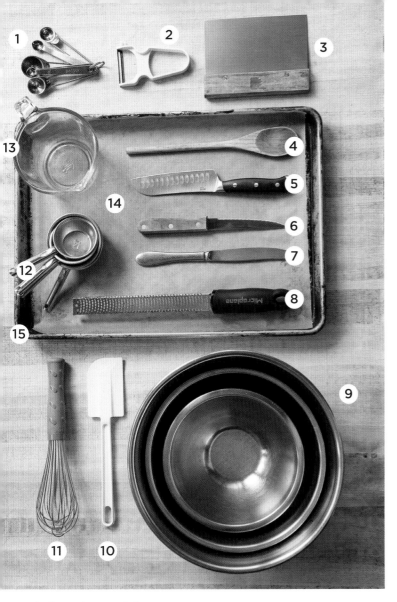

*Clockwise from top left:*

*1. Measuring spoons 2. Peeler
3. Bench scraper 4. Wooden spoon
5. Small chef's knife 6. Small serrated
knife 7. Butter knife 8. Microplane zester
9. Mixing bowls 10. Spatula 11. Whisk
12. Measuring cups 13. Liquid measuring
cup 14. Parchment paper (underneath
items) 15. Rimmed baking sheet*

that contain butter, like scones and hand pies, which tend to leak butter if the ingredients aren't kept very cold before baking. If you do not have a rimmed baking sheet, create your own rim using a piece of foil with the edges turned up.

## Bench Scraper

Bench scrapers are very useful for portioning dough, moving pie crusts, and cutting butter. Bench scrapers are also easy tools for young children to use. Though they are not designed for chopping through hard things, they can cut through peeled apples and potatoes, bananas, and other soft foods. A bench scraper is especially handy when transferring sticky bread dough. You can find metal kitchen bench or dough scrapers for less than ten dollars at kitchen supply stores.

## Peeler

Peelers are sharp tools, so always remind your child that peelers have a sharp blade. Swiss-style peelers are easier for children to use, and they come in a fun variety of colors.

## Microplane Zester

I have kids use these in class for zesting citrus fruits as well as for grating things that usually require a large knife. Although the zester does contain sharp points, I have found that children are able to use this tool successfully. Accidents happen when children grate too quickly, so watch carefully to make sure that they are focusing on the task and slowing down. If you do not have a Microplane, the small holes on a box grater may be used. Mince the gratings with a knife until they are a fine consistency.

## Knives

As mentioned in the safety chapter, children should use different knives depending on their age and experience. Small children should start using butter knives to chop soft ingredients like bananas, strawberries, and peeled apples or pears. Once children have mastered using a butter knife, they can move on to using a serrated knife.

Once children have mastered the serrated knife, they can move on to paring knives. Make sure that it is easy to tell which side of the paring knife is the sharp side and which is the dull side.

Older children can use smaller chef's knives. Include children in the buying process. Let them handle the knife at the store, and ask them which feels best in their hands. Knives that are too large will be more difficult to manage.

## Mixing Utensils

Because these recipes are all hands-on and do not use electric mixers, you will need sturdy mixing utensils. Wooden spoons are great for mixing; just be sure to wash them by hand. Small whisks are easier for children to use than large whisks. To remove batters and dough from bowls, a rubber spatula is helpful for getting every last drop.

## Bowls

You'll need small, medium, and large mixing bowls to make the recipes in this book. I choose metal bowls over glass for safety reasons. A few additional small prep bowls make it easy for children to organize their minced and measured ingredients.

## Parchment Paper

I line baking sheets with natural parchment paper, which makes removing food and cleanup easy. If you are concerned about wasting paper products, you can also invest in a silicone baking mat or two.

## Measuring Cups and Spoons

There are measuring cups for dry ingredients and for liquid ingredients. Liquid measuring cups are better for measuring liquids because you must fill dry measuring cups all the way to the top. If you (or your child) measure a liquid all the way to the top of a dry measuring cup, you are likely to spill some before making it to the mixing bowl. Choose liquid measuring cups that are easy to read. For dry ingredients, choose a set of metal measuring cups that have the size engraved on the handle. The labeling on plastic measuring cups wears off with age, making it more difficult to choose the proper size.

# PANTRY INGREDIENTS

The recipes in this book were tested with the ingredients that I am most comfortable cooking with. I tend to land on the natural side of things, using less refined cane sugar and sourcing local products. That said, there are some drawbacks to going all-natural while baking. For instance, some natural powdered sugars aren't perfectly white, making your vanilla buttercream frosting look perhaps a bit different than what you are used to. Personally, I'm okay with certain recipes not looking exactly like store-bought or professional versions of baked goods, so I often opt for the natural products. Decide for yourself and your family how you'd like to purchase ingredients. I give my two cents on my favorites here.

## Flour

Most recipes in this book call for a blend of all-purpose flour and white whole wheat flour. Whole wheat not only boosts the nutritional value of these snacks but also adds depth of flavor. Whole wheat has a nutty flavor that complements the roasted baked goods, which works perfectly for the cracker recipes. White whole wheat flour, which can be found in most grocery stores, is milder in flavor than 100 percent whole wheat flour, both in texture and in flavor.

## Sugar

I use natural cane sugar when I bake. I don't mind if a little bit of molasses clings to the sugar. I'd take that over the extra refining to make it perfectly white. That said, it takes a little longer to dissolve than white sugar, so keep that in mind. Of course there are exceptions to every rule, and the vanilla cupcakes are one of those recipes that requires white granulated sugar.

## Salt

When creating the recipes in this book, I used Diamond brand kosher salt. This is the salt I used in culinary school, and I feel most comfortable seasoning with it because I am used to the granule size. Keep in mind that table salt tastes "saltier" than kosher salt. If you are using table salt, use only half the amount of salt called for in the recipes.

Kosher salt is easier to sprinkle.

### Salt Conversion

2 teaspoons kosher salt = 1 teaspoon table salt

## Butter

In most recipes, I use butter instead of margarine or shortening. In my opinion, butter tastes better! The butter used in these recipes is unsalted butter. Salted butter is great for slathering on bread, but for baking, using unsalted butter gives you more control over the amount of salt added.

## Spices

Spices should be fragrant. Spices lose flavor with age, so if they have been sitting in your pantry for years, it's time to buy new ones. Replace spices every two to three years. Whole spices will keep for a year or so longer than their ground counterparts.

# Chapter 3

# BAKING TECHNIQUES *and* TERMS

*Help younger children with rolling out dough.*

When reading a recipe, there are often terms in the instructions like *folding* or *creaming* that the average home cook may not understand. In this section, I define some of the more common terms used in baking recipes so that when you see them, you will understand what they mean and why they are important.

## MEASURING

### Flour

The most precise way to measure flour is to use a scale and weigh your ingredients. This is particularly important for flour because it compacts as it sits in a container in your pantry.

*Scoop the flour and spoon it into the measuring cup.*

*Place a heaping mound over the measuring cup.*

*Use a butter knife to level it off.*

Because most families do not have a scale, the next best way to measure flour is to scoop the flour with a spoon and pour it into a measuring cup. Fill it up to the point of creating a mound, and then use the flat side of a butter knife to scrape the excess back into the container (not your mixing bowl!). Your dry measuring cup should be filled all the way to the top and the surface of the flour should be level with the top of the cup.

*Scoop sugar and salt directly with a measuring spoon.*

## Other Dry Ingredients

Salt, sugar, and all other dry ingredients can be measured like flour, except that you can simply scoop from the container and flatten off with a butter knife.

## Liquid

When measuring liquid, use a liquid measuring cup placed on a flat surface. Be sure to fill it up to the correct line, and double-check your measurement by looking at it from the side at eye level.

Get at eye level to measure liquids.

*Tap the egg gently on a flat surface.*

*Use your thumbs to pry apart the two sides.*

*Let the egg whites fall out and pass the yolk between the shell.*

# CRACKING EGGS

This is one baking task that has big mess potential. During my classes, no matter how many times I tell children to gently tap the egg on the table and carefully pull the two halves away from each other, most kids usually end up crushing it in their hands. Perhaps they don't realize their own strength, but it seems that learning firsthand that crushing eggs results in an egg explosion, sending bits of eggshell into the batter, is more effective than an adult explaining it over and over again. In any case, have children crack their first eggs over a separate bowl in case any shells fall in. In fact, it's a good idea to have them use a separate bowl until they've gotten the hang of it.

1 To crack an egg, tap the egg gently against the table or side of the bowl until a small crack forms. (A)

2 While holding the egg over a bowl, have children place their thumbs on either side of the crack and pull the egg apart. (B) The egg will fall out easily if the shells are pulled away from each other. Check the bowl for any shell bits before pouring the egg(s) into your batter or dough.

## Separating Eggs

To separate eggs, gather two bowls, one for your whites and one for your yolks. Tap the egg gently against the table or side of the bowl until a small crack forms. Hold the eggs so that the pointier end faces up. Over a bowl, place your thumbs on either side of the crack and pull the egg apart vertically, removing the top like it is a hat. The whites will fall out and the yolk will stay in the shell. To get the last little bits of whites, transfer the yolk back and forth between the two shell halves. (C) If a little bit of egg white gets into the yolk, it's not the end of the world. But if a little bit of yolk gets into the whites, it will prevent the egg whites from foaming.

# ZESTING

The zest from citrus adds flavor without the acidity of citrus juice. It's important to note that you only want to zest the rind and not the pith. The pith is the white layer between the rind and the pulp of the fruit. Pith can have a bitter and unpleasant taste.

*Zest the rind of citrus, being careful not to zest the white pith.*

*Be sure to scrape down the sides of the bowl to incorporate all the ingredients.*

## The Two-Spoon Method for Cookies and Batters

Use two metal spoons to portion out cookie dough and batters. Use one spoon to scoop the correct amount of dough and the other spoon to scrape it off onto the baking sheet or into the muffin cup. To avoid messes, make sure that children position the spoon directly over the cookie sheet or muffin cup before they begin to scrape it off.

# CREAMING

Creaming refers to mixing together sugars and fats (usually butter) until the mixture is lighter in color and fluffy. Use a wooden spoon or rubber spatula to mix, being sure to scrape down the sides of the bowl to incorporate all the ingredients.

Kneading develops the gluten in flour.

A. Sprinkle a small amount of flour to prevent sticking.
B. Flatten the dough with your hands.
C. Fold the dough over on itself and push it away from you with the palms of your hands.

# FOLDING

Use this technique when you are combining an ingredient with a mixture into which you have whipped air, such as egg whites. *Folding* means to combine gently enough to preserve the air bubbles in the original mixture while evenly distributing the new ingredients. Think of gently combining the batter in the same way you would fold clothes, taking the whipped mixture from one side of the bowl and placing it over the ingredients you are adding. A rubber spatula works best for this job.

*To preserve the air whipped into egg whites, gently fold them into the batter with a rubber spatula.*

# KNEADING

Why do you need to knead? Kneading develops the gluten in breads so that the dough can stretch and rise during the proofing period and while it is baking in the oven. Begin by lightly flouring your work surface. Your work surface can be a large wooden cutting board with a damp towel underneath, a wooden butcher block, or a table covered with parchment paper or a silicone mat. Whichever surface you choose, make sure it is sturdy and secure!

Remove your dough from the bowl. It may feel very sticky; if it is too sticky to handle, lightly dust your hands with flour. Push the heel of your hand down into the dough and away from you. Fold the dough in half, and then rotate the dough 90 degrees. Repeating this step over and over is called kneading, and you will need to knead your dough for about 10 minutes, or for the amount of time specified in the recipe. If you get tired before 10 minutes is up, have someone else continue kneading.

Kneading should be a rhythmic process; do not go too slow or you will not have kneaded enough, and the bread will turn out tough and dense. The dough is ready when it is shiny, holds its shape, and is no longer sticky. Shape the dough into a ball and it is ready to proof!

# PROOFING DOUGH

Proofing is a period of time when dough for a leavened bread (meaning bread made using yeast) is left to rest in order to rise and expand. The recipe may say to proof the dough for an hour. This means place the dough in a lightly oiled bowl, cover it with plastic wrap or a plate, and allow it to sit undisturbed until it has doubled in size. You want to proof the dough in a warm, draft-free place where it won't get moved around.

# Chapter 4

# Healthy BREAKFAST BAKED GOODS

Rise & Shine!

## recipe box

### SEASONAL MUFFINS

Spring: Roasted Strawberry Muffins

Summer: Blueberry Muffins

Fall: Pumpkin Spice Muffins

Winter: Lemon Poppy Seed Muffins

### SEASONAL SCONES

Spring: Savory Cheddar and Spring Onion Scones

Summer: Blackberry Scones

Fall: Apple Pie Scones

Winter: Orange Pomegranate Scones

Easy Drop Biscuits

# MORNINGS CAN BE STRESSFUL

**Getting the kids dressed and fed can feel like a daunting task. Instead of hitting up a coffee shop or buying premade pastries and breakfast bars for sustenance, I encourage you to bake your own. You might be asking yourself, "Who has the time for that?"**

Sure, stopping in your local coffee shop or buying premade breakfast bars for a quick breakfast *is* easy. I will argue, though, that the scones and muffins in most coffee shops are large, expensive, and usually topped with a sugary glaze. And, many prepackaged breakfast bars contain ingredients your children could do without. By baking your own scones and muffins ahead of time, you can save money, control the portion size and sugar content, and even sneak in vitamin-rich fruits and whole wheat flour. Take a look in your pantry and you may be surprised by how many ready-to-use ingredients you already have!

Scones and muffins can be baked on the weekend and kept in the freezer for weekday breakfasts on the go. Wrap the baked goods individually in foil and then with plastic wrap. Remove muffins or scones from the freezer the night before and you'll have homemade pastries ready for you in the morning!

In this chapter you will find quick and easy breakfast goodies that incorporate fresh, seasonal fruit—perfect for satisfying you and your family on those rushed weekday mornings.

## Seasonal Muffins

Muffins are a great way to incorporate seasonal flavors. In this section you'll find a muffin recipe for every season, each utilizing fresh fruits and spices to complement the season's bounty!

### Don't Have Buttermilk?

Don't sweat it! Here are some handy substitutes for buttermilk.

For 1 cup (235 ml) buttermilk:

2 tablespoons (30 ml) lemon juice or vinegar

1 cup (235 ml) whole, part-skim, or skim milk

OR

¾ cup (180 ml) whole, part-skim, or skim milk

¼ cup (60 g) whole, part-skim, or skim yogurt

## Seasonal Scones

Scones are delicious and buttery, and, like muffins, provide a great platform for adding seasonal fruits to the first meal of the day. The possibilities are endless. In fact, this section even includes a recipe for a savory scone that incorporates veggies into your breakfast pastries!

*Learn about seasonality and include children in picking out fruits and vegetables.*

*When children help buy produce at the market, they are gaining valuable life skills and can practice math.*

*Bring your children to the market.*

## Teaching Kids about Seasonality

One of the best ways to teach your children about eating foods that are in season is by visiting your local farmers' market. The Slow Food movement has brought farmers' markets to most cities. Farmers' market shopping titillates the senses—the colors are vibrant, the food is fresh and fragrant, and most farmers are happy to provide samples of their bounty. Farmers' markets also typically feature live music from local bands and are very family-friendly. By supporting your local farmers' market, you are supporting your local economy and helping to build a sense of community. The Noe Valley Farmers' Market is one of my very favorite places to take kids in San Francisco. And, when I'm visiting other cities and regions, I find that a trip to the local farmers' market gives me a better understanding of the culture, allowing me to see, taste, and smell the foods that grow there.

Each month at my cooking school, I take a group of young children to tour the nearby farmers' market to teach them about farms and to pick out food. Instead of lecturing children about which fruits and vegetables are in season, I find that showing them leaves a more lasting impression. I make tours of the market fun by creating scavenger hunts, encouraging the children to look for each color of the rainbow in the fruits and vegetables displayed, and by allowing the children to ask the farmers questions. When children are given the freedom to purchase ingredients themselves and count their own money, they also learn social and math skills, which makes the trip a rewarding and confidence-boosting experience for them.

Bring your kids to the farmers' market to help procure groceries and you'll be surprised by how many new foods they're likely to try! Spending time at the farmers' market together can inspire creative kids to cook new cuisines, too.

## ingredients

**For Roasted Strawberries:**
- ~ 3 cups (510 g) hulled and quartered fresh strawberries
- ~ 1 tablespoon (12 g) sugar

**For Muffins:**
- ~ 5 tablespoons (70 g) unsalted butter, softened
- ~ ½ cup (100 g) sugar
- ~ 1 large egg
- ~ ½ cup (120 g) whole milk yogurt
- ~ ½ teaspoon lemon zest
- ~ 1 cup (120 g) all-purpose flour
- ~ ½ cup (60 g) white whole wheat flour
- ~ 1½ teaspoons baking powder
- ~ ¼ teaspoon baking soda
- ~ ½ teaspoon salt
- ~ roasted strawberries (from above)

# Spring: Roasted
# STRAWBERRY MUFFINS

Roasting the strawberries ahead of time is crucial to this recipe; otherwise, the strawberries add too much moisture to the muffin and end up with a slimy texture. Roasting strawberries concentrates their flavor and brings out their natural sweetness. The strawberry puree makes these muffins a lovely shade of pink, and they would make a delicious moist cupcake with some vanilla buttercream.

*Yield:* **12** *muffins*

## tools needed

- ~ measuring cups and spoons
- ~ liquid measuring cup
- ~ Microplane zester
- ~ large bowl
- ~ medium bowl
- ~ standard-size 12-cup muffin tin
- ~ muffin liners
- ~ 2 rimmed baking sheets
- ~ parchment paper
- ~ whisk
- ~ wooden spoon or spatula
- ~ butter knife

### for smaller hands

Strawberries are quite easy to cut with a butter knife. Have children pull off the green before slicing off the stem. Use the bridge technique (see page 12) to cut the berries in half, then place flat sides down and cut in half again lengthwise. ~

# INSTRUCTIONS

1 Preheat the oven to 375°F (190°C, or gas mark 5). Prepare the muffin tin with paper liners and set aside. Children like to help out with this step—just make sure to show them how to separate the paper liners to avoid wasting them!

*Younger children can easily slice strawberries with a butter knife.*

Use the bridge technique to halve the strawberries.

*Roast the berries until the liquid is syrupy around the edges.*

### for smaller hands

Make sure children know not to touch baking pans because they can be hot. Set a rule to never touch baked goods when they are still on the baking sheet. Let children know that it's time to taste test when baked goods have been placed on a special plate or tray. ~

3 Use a wooden spoon to cream together the butter and sugar in a large bowl until light and fluffy. If the butter is difficult to mix, soften it in the microwave. Place it in a microwave-safe bowl and microwave for about 15 seconds. If the butter is not yet soft, heat for an additional 15 seconds, until the butter is soft but not melted.

4 Add the egg and beat well. Add the yogurt, strawberry puree, and lemon zest.

5 With a clean, dry whisk, mix together both flours, baking powder, baking soda, and salt in a separate bowl. Stir half of the flour mixture into the butter mixture. Mix until just combined. Pour the remaining dry ingredients into the batter and mix just until the flour disappears into the batter. Very gently fold in the roasted strawberries, to keep them intact. The batter will be quite thick.

### for smaller hands

Explain to your child the importance of gently mixing the flour in this recipe just enough to bring it together. While mixing is fun, dense, tough muffins are not! ~

2 For the strawberries, line a baking sheet with parchment paper and toss together the strawberries and sugar. Spread out the strawberries in a single layer and roast for 15 to 20 minutes, or until most of the liquid has evaporated and the juices surrounding the strawberries become syrupy. Remove the pan from the oven and allow to cool to room temperature. To make pink muffins, use a hand blender or small food processor to puree a scant ½ cup (85 g) of roasted strawberries and set aside. You could also mash the berries with a fork while still warm. If you would rather not have pink muffins, skip the pureeing step and simply fold in all the berries at the end.

If there is more than one child participating in cooking, have each stir ten times before passing it along, or have one child mix in the egg, and one child mix in the yogurt, switching off for the strawberry puree and zest. If children become restless while the other child is mixing, have them take turns holding the bowl for the person who is mixing. It reinforces teamwork and keeps all the children busy! ~

6 Fill each muffin cup about three-fourths full. (See page 23 for tips on how to fill muffin cups using the two-spoon method.) Bake for 15 to 25 minutes, checking and rotating the pans after 12 minutes. When the muffins are done, the tops will be golden and a wooden skewer inserted into the center of a muffin will come out clean.

7 Let the muffins cool in the pan for 5 minutes and then transfer to a cooling rack to cool completely.

Mixing is easier when someone holds the bowl!

HEALTHY BREAKFAST BAKED GOODS

## ingredients

- ~ 5 tablespoons (70 g) unsalted butter, softened
- ~ ½ cup (100 g) sugar
- ~ 1 large egg
- ~ ¾ cup (180 g) whole milk yogurt
- ~ ½ teaspoon lemon zest
- ~ 1 cup (120 g) all-purpose flour
- ~ ½ cup (60 g) white whole wheat flour
- ~ 1½ teaspoons baking powder
- ~ ¼ teaspoon baking soda
- ~ ½ teaspoon salt
- ~ ¾ cup (110 g) blueberries

*Summer:*

# BLUEBERRY MUFFINS

Blueberry muffins are a classic crowd-pleaser, and this version is brightened up with lemon zest, which adds depth of flavor.

*Yield:*  **12** *muffins*

## tools needed

~ measuring cups and spoons
~ liquid measuring cup
~ large bowl
~ medium bowl
~ wooden spoon or spatula
~ Microplane zester
~ standard-size 12-cup muffin tin
~ muffin liners
~ whisk

If your family has a hankering for blueberry muffins in the fall, winter, or spring, opt for frozen blueberries instead of fresh blueberries grown far away. Frozen berries are an excellent choice because they are picked at peak flavor and frozen immediately. Fresh berries that need to be shipped long distances during the off-season lack flavor because they are picked before they are ripe to lengthen shelf life. Frozen blueberries do not need to be thawed before adding to this recipe.

# INSTRUCTIONS

1 Preheat the oven to 375°F (190°C, or gas mark 5). Line a muffin tin with 12 paper liners. Children like to help out with this step—just be sure to show them how to separate the paper liners to avoid wasting them!

2 In a large mixing bowl, use a wooden spoon to cream together the butter and sugar until light and fluffy. (A) If the butter is difficult to mix, microwave it in a microwave-safe bowl for 15 seconds and try again.

### for smaller hands

If there is more than one child mixing, have them each stir ten times before passing it along. ~

### for smaller hands

Cracking eggs for young ones is either very exciting or very yucky. In any case, children most often crush the egg instead of cracking it in half and pulling the two sides apart. With supervision, I let children crack the eggs in class over a separate bowl to catch any egg implosions. (See page 22 for more detailed instructions.) Be sure to let children know about the risk of contamination when handling raw eggs; tell them not to touch anything until they have washed their hands. ~

3 Add the egg and beat well, then add the yogurt and zest.

*Butter and sugar are creamed together.*

4 In a separate medium-size mixing bowl, use a clean, dry whisk to mix together the flours, baking powder, baking soda, and salt. Stir half of the flour mixture into the butter mixture. Mix until just combined. Add the dry ingredients to the batter and mix just until the flour disappears. Gently fold in the blueberries. (B) The batter will be quite thick. Remind children to gently mix, or the muffins will be dense and tough.

Gently
fold in the
blueberries.

5 Fill each muffin cup about three-fourths full.
(See page 23 for tips on how to fill muffin
cups using the two-spoon method.)

## for smaller hands

Fill one muffin cup up for your child to
use as an example when filling the muffin
cups themselves. You can always scoop out
a little from each muffin cup if some are
filled more than others. ~

6 Bake for 15 to 25 minutes, rotating the pan
after 12 minutes. The muffins are done
when the tops are a light golden color and
a tester inserted into the center of the
muffin comes out clean.

7 Let the muffins cool in the pan for 5 minutes, and then transfer to a cooling rack
to cool completely.

## for smaller hands

Remind children never to touch baked
goods when they are still on the baking
sheet. They will know it's time to taste test
when the muffins are moved to a special
plate or tray. ~

## ingredients

- ~ 1 cup (120 g) all-purpose flour
- ~ ½ cup (60 g) white whole wheat flour
- ~ 1 teaspoon baking powder
- ~ ½ teaspoon baking soda
- ~ 1 teaspoon salt
- ~ 1½ teaspoons pumpkin-pie spice
- ~ 1⅓ cups (325 g) fresh roasted pumpkin puree or canned pumpkin puree
- ~ 5 tablespoons (70 g) unsalted butter, melted
- ~ 2 large eggs
- ~ 1¼ cups (250 g) sugar

**For Cinnamon Sugar Topping:**
- ~ 1 tablespoon (12 g) sugar
- ~ 1 teaspoon ground cinnamon

*Fall:*
# PUMPKIN SPICE MUFFINS

To me, the smell of roasting pumpkin and warm spices coming from the kitchen is a quintessential sign of fall.

*Yield:*  *12 muffins*

## tools needed

- measuring cups and spoons
- liquid measuring cup
- medium bowl
- large bowl
- jar with lid
- standard-size 12-cup muffin tin
- muffin liners
- whisk
- wooden spoon or spatula

These muffins are great for beginning bakers because they are delicious and very easy to prepare. Turn these muffins into a decadent dessert by topping them with a luscious cream cheese frosting.

# INSTRUCTIONS

**1** Preheat the oven to 350°F (180°C, or gas mark 4). Fill the muffin tin with paper liners. Children like to help out with this step—just be sure to show them how to separate the papers to avoid wasting them!

**2** In a medium-size mixing bowl, whisk together the flours, baking powder, baking soda, salt, and spice until thoroughly combined. Set aside.

### for smaller hands

Avoid arguments by having the kids take turns. Ask one child to pour in ingredients while the other child mixes them in. It is fun to add the spice mixture and watch it change the color of the flour from white to golden brown. ～

**3** In a separate large mixing bowl, whisk together the pumpkin puree, butter, eggs, and sugar.

### for smaller hands

Explain to your child the importance of gently mixing the flour in this recipe just enough to bring it together. While mixing is fun, dense, chewy muffins are not! It is especially easy to overmix these muffins because the batter is thinner than other batters in this chapter. ～

4 Stir half of the flour mixture into the pumpkin mixture. (A) Mix until just combined. Pour the remaining dry ingredients into the batter and mix just until the flour is no longer visible.

5 For the topping, in a small jar with a lid, combine the sugar and cinnamon. Shake to mix.

### for smaller hands

A great chef taught me how to season food properly. Season from up high, so that whatever you are sprinkling is dispersed more evenly. If you season food really close, the seasoning lands on the food in clumps, making each bite inconsistent. The same idea can be applied here. Sprinkle from 1 to 2 feet (30 to 60 cm) above the muffins so that the cinnamon sugar is dispersed evenly. ~

6 Fill each muffin cup about three-fourths full. (See page 23 for tips on how to fill muffin cups using the two-spoon method.) Sprinkle a little of the topping over each muffin before baking. (B)

7 Bake for 15 to 25 minutes, checking the muffins and rotating the pan after 12 minutes. The muffins are done when they are golden brown and a wooden skewer inserted into the center comes out clean.

8 Let the muffins cool in the pan for 5 minutes, and then transfer to a cooling rack to cool completely.

A

*Add the mixed dry ingredients to the wet.*

### for smaller hands

Adults should always pull out muffins and test for doneness, not young children. To avoid accidents, make sure that children are a safe distance away when removing hot pans from the oven. ~

Sprinkle a little topping evenly over each muffin.

## ingredients

- ~ 1 medium lemon
- ~ ⅔ cup (132 g) cane sugar
- ~ 1 cup (120 g) all-purpose flour
- ~ ½ cup (60 g) white whole wheat flour
- ~ 2 teaspoons baking powder
- ~ ¼ teaspoon baking soda
- ~ ¼ teaspoon salt
- ~ 2 large eggs
- ~ ¾ cup (180 ml) buttermilk*
- ~ 1 teaspoon pure vanilla extract
- ~ 1 stick (½ cup, or 112 g) unsalted butter, melted and cooled
- ~ 2 tablespoons (12 g) poppy seeds

**For Lemon Sugar Topping:**
- ~ 2 tablespoons (24 g) cane sugar
- ~ 1 teaspoon lemon zest

*Who always has buttermilk on hand? Not me
See page 27 for buttermilk substitutions.*

*Winter: Lemon*
# POPPY SEED MUFFINS

These muffins, sunny and bright from the lemon juice and zest, are a perfect way to start off your morning. The tiny poppy seeds, which lend a pretty flecked look and texture to the muffin, add a delightful slight crunch to each bite.

Yield:  12 muffins

## tools needed

~ measuring cups and spoons
~ liquid measuring cup
~ large bowl
~ medium bowl
~ 2 small bowls
~ Microplane zester
~ citrus juicer
~ standard-size 12-cup muffin tin
~ muffin liners
~ whisk
~ wooden spoon or spatula
~ knife

*Pinch the lemon zest into the sugar to release the oils from the rind.*

# INSTRUCTIONS

**1** Preheat the oven to 400°F (200°C, or gas mark 6). Fill the muffin tin with paper liners. Children like to help out with this step—just be sure to show them how to separate the papers to avoid wasting them!

### for smaller hands

Step 3 is aromatic and it's magical the way the lemon zest turns the sugar yellow! Use your fingertips to release the lemon oils from the zest by pinching the sugar and lemon zest together. ~

**2** Zest the lemon over a small bowl using a Microplane. Then, juice the lemon with a citrus juicer over another small bowl so that you can pick out any seeds that end up on in the juice. Children can easily help with this step. If half of a lemon is too difficult for your children to juice, try cutting it into quarters.

**3** In a medium bowl, rub the sugar with the lemon zest until the sugar is yellow and scented with lemon. (A)

Muffins are done when a toothpick inserted in the center comes out clean.

4 Whisk the flours, baking powder, baking soda, and salt into the sugar and lemon zest mixture. In a separate large bowl, whisk together the eggs, buttermilk, vanilla, melted butter, and lemon juice.

### for smaller hands

For many baking recipes, the dry ingredients are kept separate from the wet ingredients until the very end. This is an important step because you do not want to overmix the flour once liquid has been added, or your baked goods may become tough. This recipe is unique in that you add the sugar directly to the flour mixture. ~

5 Stir half of the flour mixture into the buttermilk mixture. Mix until just combined. Pour the remaining dry ingredients into the batter and mix just until the flour is no longer visible. Gently fold in the poppy seeds, taking care not to overmix.

6 For the lemon sugar topping, as in step 3, rub the sugar with the lemon zest until the sugar is yellow and fragrant.

### for smaller hands

Fill one muffin cup three-fourths full for children to use as a guide when filling the muffin cups themselves. You can always scoop out a little from each muffin cup if some are filled more than others. ~

7 Fill the muffin cups about three-fourths full. (See page 23 for tips on how to fill muffin cups using the two-spoon method.) Sprinkle each muffin with the lemon sugar.

8 Bake for 15 to 20 minutes, rotating the pan halfway through. The muffins are done when the tops are golden and a toothpick inserted into the center comes out clean.

9 Let the muffins cool in the pan for 5 minutes, and then transfer to a cooling rack to cool completely.

## ingredients

- ~ 1½ cups (180 g) all-purpose flour
- ~ ½ cup (60 g) white whole wheat flour
- ~ 1 tablespoon (8 g) baking powder
- ~ ½ teaspoon salt
- ~ 6 tablespoons (84 g) cold unsalted butter, cut into pieces
- ~ 1 cup (120 g) grated sharp Cheddar cheese
- ~ 1 to 3 spring or green onions, cleaned, trimmed, and thinly sliced (both white and green parts, about ¾ cup [75 g] total)
- ~ ⅓ cup (80 ml) buttermilk*

*Who always has buttermilk on hand? Not me! See page 27 for buttermilk substitutions.*

## Spring: Savory Cheddar and
# SPRING ONION SCONES

This twist on a scone borders on a savory biscuit—they are moist, delicious, and perfect with scrambled eggs. If you are having a hard time finding spring onions, green onions will work just as well.

Yield: **8-12** scones

## tools needed

~ measuring cups and spoons

~ liquid measuring cup

~ large mixing bowl

~ medium bowl

~ cheese grater

~ baking sheet

~ parchment paper

~ whisk

~ knife or bench scraper

~ wooden spoon or spatula

~ cookie or biscuit cutters (optional)

### for smaller hands

Children can grate cheese with supervision. Have them hold the cheese with their fingers curled, much like when chopping. Instruct the children to grate slowly to prevent accidents. When the cheese piece is very small and hard to handle, tell them to stop and ask an adult to finish. ~

# INSTRUCTIONS

1 Preheat the oven to 375°F (190°C, or gas mark 5). Line a baking sheet with parchment paper and set aside.

2 In a large mixing bowl, whisk together the flours, baking powder, and salt. Add the butter and toss it with the flour until the butter is completely coated. Using a pastry cutter, 2 butter knives, or your fingertips, cut the butter into the flour until the mixture is crumbly with pea-size chunks. Do not overmix.

*Kids can help grate cheese if they grate carefully and slowly.*

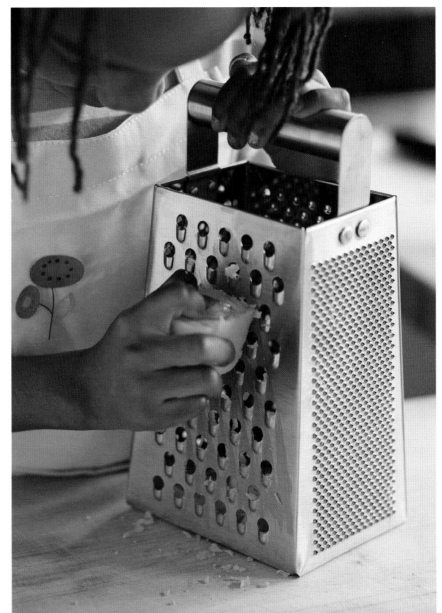

Shape and flatten the dough.

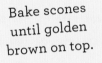

Bake scones until golden brown on top.

3 Gently toss in the Cheddar cheese and spring onions. Stir in the buttermilk until just blended. Do not overmix.

4 Sprinkle a light dusting of flour over the work surface and turn out the dough.

5 Flatten the dough until it is about 1½ inches (3.8 cm) thick. (A) Cut the scones into triangles or squares, or use cookie or biscuit cutters. Once you have cut the scones, combine the scraps gently and cut out more scones. Note that smaller scones will take less time to bake. Place the scones onto the prepared baking sheet.

6 Bake for 15 to 20 minutes, or until golden brown on top. (B) Allow to cool for 5 minutes before transferring the scones to a serving dish.

### for smaller hands

Children love to use cookie cutters to cut out dough. To avoid overworking the dough, show them how to arrange the cutters to make the best use of the first round of dough. ∼

HEALTHY BREAKFAST BAKED GOODS

## ingredients

- ~ 1 cup (145 g) fresh or frozen blackberries
- ~ 1¼ cups (150 g) all-purpose flour
- ~ ½ cup (60 g) white whole wheat flour
- ~ ½ cup (100 g) sugar
- ~ 1½ teaspoons baking powder
- ~ 1 teaspoon baking soda
- ~ ½ teaspoon salt
- ~ 1 stick (½ cup, or 112 g) cold unsalted butter, cubed
- ~ 2 teaspoons pure vanilla extract
- ~ ½ cup (120 ml) buttermilk*

**For Egg Wash:**
- ~ 1 large egg, beaten
- ~ 1 tablespoon (15 ml) water

- ~ 2 tablespoons (24 g) sugar, for sprinkling

*Who always has buttermilk on hand? Not me! See page 27 for buttermilk substitutions.*

*Summer:*

# BLACKBERRY SCONES

These tender, buttery scones pair perfectly with the blackberry, one of the juiciest berries of the summer season. As the scones bake, the tart and sweet berries melt into warm, jammy pockets, making these treats a satisfying and hearty way to begin your day.

*Yield:*  **8-12** scones

## tools needed

~ measuring cups and spoons
~ liquid measuring cup
~ medium bowl
~ 2 rimmed baking sheets
~ tray or baking sheet that fits inside your freezer
~ parchment paper
~ whisk
~ knife or bench scraper
~ wooden spoon or spatula
~ cookie or biscuit cutters (optional)

Use a bench scraper to cube the butter.

# INSTRUCTIONS

**1** Preheat the oven to 375°F (190°C, or gas mark 5). Line a baking sheet with parchment paper and set aside. If you are using frozen berries, skip to step 3.

**2** Flash-freeze fresh berries to prevent them from breaking apart in the dough. Line a second baking sheet with parchment paper and scatter the berries in a single layer. Freeze for about 1 hour, or until the berries have hardened.

**3** In a medium mixing bowl, whisk together the flours, sugar, baking powder, baking soda, and salt. Sprinkle the cubes of butter onto the flour and toss gently until the butter cubes are coated with flour. Using a pastry cutter, 2 butter knives, or your fingertips, cut the butter into the flour mixture until it is crumbly (A) with some visible pieces of butter throughout.

*Pinch the butter into the flour with your fingertips or two butter knives.*

### for smaller hands

Have kids blend the butter into the flour with two butter knives or by pinching the butter and flour with their fingertips. But make sure they don't overmix the dough or squeeze the dough between their fingers, which causes the butter to warm up. Both will result in a tough, dense scone. ~

4 Stir in the vanilla and buttermilk until just blended, then fold in the frozen berries, being careful not to smash them (although if they break up slightly it's not a big deal). Do not overmix.

### for smaller hands

Children can help pour the milk and mix, but be careful not to overmix the dough! Have children stop mixing when they cannot see any more flour. ~

5 Lightly flour the work surface.

6 Turn the dough out onto the work surface. Flatten the dough until it is about 1½ inches (3.8 cm) thick. Use a bench scraper to cut your scones into triangles or squares, or use cookie or biscuit cutters (B) to shape the scones. Gently combine the leftover scraps, flatten the dough, and cut more scones. Note that smaller scones will take less time to bake.

### for smaller hands

Show children how to sprinkle a small amount of flour over the work surface. It should look like a light dusting of snow, not a blizzard. ~

7 For the egg wash, mix together the egg and water. Place the scones onto the prepared baking sheet. Using a pastry brush, brush the egg wash on the tops of the scones. Sprinkle the sugar on the scones and bake for 15 to 20 minutes, or until golden. Allow to cool for 5 minutes and then transfer to a serving dish.

Cut out the scones using cookie cutters or a bench scraper.

### for smaller hands

Have children use cookie cutters to cut out dough. Help them figure out how many scones they can cut at a time to avoid overworking the dough. ~

## ingredients

### For Roasted Apples:
~ 2 small apples (Fuji, Granny Smith, or any tart-sweet apple)
~ 1 tablespoon (12 g) sugar
~ ½ teaspoon ground cinnamon
~ zest of 1 lemon

### For Scone Dough:
~ 1 cup (120 g) all-purpose flour
~ ¾ cup (90 g) white whole wheat flour
~ 4 teaspoons baking powder
~ ¼ cup (50 g) cane sugar
~ ½ teaspoon salt
~ 5 tablespoons (70 g) cold unsalted butter, cut into small chunks
~ ¾ cup (180 ml) buttermilk*

### For Egg Wash:
~ 1 large egg
~ 1 tablespoon (15 ml) water

~ 2 tablespoons (24 g) sugar, for sprinkling

*Who always has buttermilk on hand? Not me! See page 27 for buttermilk substitutions.*

# Fall: APPLE PIE SCONES

These scones take the buttery, cinnamon-spiced flavors of apple pie and transform them into a delicious breakfast confection.

Yield:  8-12 *scones*

## tools needed

measuring cups and spoons

liquid measuring cup

large bowl

medium bowl

Microplane zester

2 baking sheets

parchment paper

peeler

knife or bench scraper

whisk

wooden spoon or spatula

cookie or biscuit cutters (optional)

**Roasting the apples caramelizes them and adds a warm layer of flavor that you wouldn't get from raw apples. The lemon zest brings out the tartness of the apples, providing a nice balance of flavors.**

A

# INSTRUCTIONS

1 Preheat the oven to 400°F (200°C, or gas mark 6). Line 2 baking sheets with parchment paper and set aside.

2 For the roasted apples, peel, core, and chop the apples into ½-inch (1.3 cm) dice. Place on one of the prepared baking sheets and toss with the sugar, cinnamon, and lemon zest. Place in the oven and roast until the edges are slightly golden, about 15 minutes. (A) Allow to cool completely.

### for smaller hands

Children can peel apples, but remind them about peeling away from their hand. Cut the apple off the core for younger children, and have them chop the larger pieces into cubes. Large slices of peeled apples can be chopped into cubes with ease using a bench scraper or a butter knife. ~

*Roast the apples until they are golden on the edges.*

**3** For the scone dough, in a large mixing bowl, whisk together the flours, baking powder, sugar, and salt. Add the butter and toss it with the flour until the butter cubes are completely coated. Using a pastry cutter, 2 butter knives, or your fingertips, cut the butter into the flour until the mixture is crumbly with visible pea-size chunks of butter. Gently mix in the cooled apples.

**4** Stir in the buttermilk until just blended. Do not overmix.

### for smaller hands

Children can help pour the milk and mix, but remind them not to overmix the dough! Explain to children to stop mixing when they cannot see any more flour. ∼

**5** Sprinkle a light dusting of flour over your work surface.

### for smaller hands

Instruct children on flouring the work surface. Show them how to sprinkle a small amount of flour. It should look like a light dusting of snow, not a blizzard. ∼

**6** Turn out the dough onto your work surface. Flatten the dough until it is about 1½ inches (3.8 cm) thick. Cut your scones into triangles or squares, or use cookie or biscuit cutters. Gently combine any scraps and use them to cut out more scones. Note that smaller scones will take less time to bake. Place the scones onto the prepared baking sheets.

### for smaller hands

If using cookie cutters, show children how to figure out how many scones they can cut at a time, to avoid overworking the dough. ∼

**7** For the egg wash, in a small bowl, whisk together the egg and water. Brush the tops of the scones with the wash and sprinkle with the sugar. Bake for 12 to 15 minutes, or until golden. Allow the scones to cool on the pan for about 5 minutes before transferring to a serving dish.

*Your dusting of flour should not look like a blizzard!*

B

Brush egg wash onto the scones for a shiny, golden color.

## ingredients

- ~ 1 cup (120 g) all-purpose flour
- ~ ¾ cup (90 g) whole wheat pastry flour
- ~ 4 teaspoons baking powder
- ~ ¼ cup (50 g) sugar
- ~ zest of 1 orange
- ~ pinch of salt
- ~ 5 tablespoons (70 g) cold unsalted butter, cut into small chunks
- ~ 2 or 3 oranges, freshly squeezed to make ½ cup (120 ml) juice (be sure to juice the one you zest!)
- ~ ¼ cup (60 g) whole milk yogurt
- ~ ¾ cup (120 g) pomegranate arils

**For Egg Wash:**
- ~ 1 large egg
- ~ 1 tablespoon (15 ml) water

*Winter: Orange*
# POMEGRANATE SCONES

**Pomegranates are filled with arils that are like ruby-red jewels.**

*Yield:*  **8-12** *scones*

## tools needed

measuring cups and spoons

liquid measuring cup

large bowl

medium bowl

small bowl

Microplane zester

citrus juicer

baking sheet

parchment paper

whisk

knife or bench scraper

wooden spoon or spatula

cookie or biscuit cutters (optional)

pastry brush

# INSTRUCTIONS

1 Preheat the oven to 400°F (200°C, or gas mark 6). Line a baking sheet with parchment paper and set aside.

2 In a large mixing bowl, whisk together the flours, baking powder, sugar, orange zest, and salt. Add the butter and toss it with the flour until the butter is completely coated. (A) Using a pastry cutter, 2 butter knives, or your fingertips, cut the butter into the flour until the mixture is crumbly with pea-size chunks. Stir in the orange juice and yogurt until just blended.

Children love to help break open the pomegranates, because it's like lifting the lid on a treasure chest. Both beautiful and tasty, pomegranates are also a great source of antioxidants. The combination of orange and pomegranates is a delicious way to utilize winter fruits.

A

Sprinkle the cubed butter into the flour.

*Gently break apart the pomegranate to reveal the jewel-like arils.*

## Removing Arils from Pomegranates

To remove the arils from a pomegranate, score the pomegranate around the diameter of the fruit. Working over a bowl to catch the red juice, pull apart the two halves. (Pomegranate juice can stain clothing and counters, so always wear an apron and work over a bowl.) Now use your fingers to gently pull the arils from the white pith of each half. They will fall out easily with little force.

### for smaller hands

Have children sprinkle the pomegranate arils evenly, and after you center the dough, have the child gently press the layers together. ~

**4** Cut your scones into triangles or squares, or use cookie or biscuit cutters. Gently combine the scraps and cut out more scones. Note that smaller scones will take less time to bake. Place the scones onto the prepared baking sheet.

### for smaller hands

Have children help cut the scones. Use a bench scraper to mark the dough with cutting guidelines to make sure the scone sizes are consistent. ~

**3** Sprinkle a light dusting of flour over the work surface and turn out the dough. Press the dough into a rectangle until it is about ½ inch (1.3 cm) thick. Cut the dough into 3 equal pieces. Into one-third of the dough, press ¼ cup (40 g) of the pomegranate arils. Press another third of the dough over the pomegranates. Sprinkle another ¼ cup (40 g) of arils over this second layer, pressing them into the dough. Add the final third of dough on top, dotting it with the remaining ¼ cup (40 g) of pomegranate arils.

**5** For the egg wash, whisk together the egg and water and brush the wash over the top of the scones. Bake for 12 to 15 minutes, or until golden. Allow to cool for 5 minutes before transferring to a serving dish.

## ingredients

~ 1½ cups (180 g) all-purpose flour
~ ½ cup (60 g) white whole wheat flour
~ 1 tablespoon (12 g) baking powder
~ 1 teaspoon kosher salt
~ 1 stick (½ cup, or 112 g) cold unsalted butter, cut into small pieces
~ 1 cup (235 ml) whole milk

## tools needed

~ measuring cups and spoons
~ liquid measuring cup
~ medium bowl
~ baking sheet
~ parchment paper
~ whisk
~ bench scraper
~ wooden spoon or spatula

# *Easy* DROP BISCUITS

Light and flaky, these biscuits are delicious as part of an elaborate breakfast feast or with simple cherry preserves (see Cherry Frosting, page 154). These biscuits are quick to prepare and because they are drop biscuits, they clean up in a cinch as well!

*Yield:* **8-10** biscuits

If the butter seems like it has softened, pop it into the freezer for 5 minutes before continuing.

# INSTRUCTIONS

1. Preheat the oven to 400°F (200°C, or gas mark 6). Line a baking sheet with parchment paper and set aside.

2. In a medium bowl, whisk together the flours, baking powder, and salt. Gently toss the butter with the flour until all the butter cubes are completely coated.

3. Using a pastry cutter, 2 butter knives, or your fingertips, cut the butter into the flour until the butter is the size of peas, being careful not to overmix. Chill in the refrigerator for 5 minutes.

## for smaller hands

Watch children as they mix because kids like to squeeze the dough between their fingers, warming it and potentially overmixing. This will result in tough and dense biscuits. ～

4. Add the milk and stir until just combined. Be careful not to overmix.

5. Using two spoons, scoop about a ¼-cup (60 g) portion of dough into mounds onto the prepared baking sheet. Bake for 18 to 20 minutes, or until golden. Allow to cool for 5 minutes before transferring to a serving dish.

*Drop the biscuits using the two-spoon method (see page 23).*

# Chapter 5

# BREADS *and* SNACKS

## recipe box

### BREADS
Hearty Soda Bread

Easy Overnight French Baguettes

### SNACKS
Honey Mustard Soft Pretzels

Fancy-Schmancy Cheesy Cheddar Puffs

Cheddar Squares

Crispy Crunchy Olive Oil Crackers

Good-for-You Graham Crackers

# WHY BAKE FROM SCRATCH?

**Homemade breads, pretzels, and crackers not only taste better than store-bought, but they also make for more rewarding meals. Baking snacks and breads is an opportunity to educate your kids about how familiar brand-name favorites are made in a real kitchen. And—it's a lot of fun.**

Bread baking is a magical process for people of all ages, and you can't beat a house filled with the smell of fresh bread rising in the oven. The Hearty Soda Bread (page 66) is a great beginner's recipe, as it takes a little under an hour from start to finish. Your work is rewarded with a delicious bread that is best eaten toasted with a smear of butter. The Easy Overnight French Baguettes (page 70) don't have the instant gratification of the soda bread recipe but is a great recipe for teaching children the art of planning ahead. Mix the ingredients before bed and wake up to dough that has magically doubled in size overnight!

The snack recipes in this chapter are not only incredibly tasty, but they also provide a fun activity for children, involving all their senses. Instead of buying play dough, have your kids help with cracker making. Set up a cracker-cutting station at the dinner table and have kids cut out shapes for crackers and place on baking sheets while you prepare dinner. Older kids can roll out dough, and younger siblings can use cookie cutters to form the crackers. It's an entertaining lesson with a nourishing result. You can make a double batch of the dough and freeze half, so kids have a hands-on project, ready to go for a rainy day. The Crispy Crunchy Olive Oil Crackers (page 88) are the most forgiving dough, as you can reroll the leftover scraps to make more crackers without sacrificing too much quality.

## A Few Long Words about Processed Foods

Have you read the ingredient list of most brand-name snacks? Thiamine mononitrate? Riboflavin? Not only are those ingredients hard to pronounce, but they are also the products of cheap processing techniques. The milling process strips most of the nutrients from flour, which is why these synthesized vitamins are added. (Remember, we are talking about ingredients used in food that are supposed to nourish us!) In addition to mystery ingredients, most store-bought snacks have a large amount of sodium. Making crackers from scratch allows you to decide how much salt you'd like your family to consume. Just watch out for kids going heavy on the finishing sprinkling of salt. On the other hand, it's important to take any advice that doesn't feel right for you and your family with a grain of you-know-what.

You'll also notice that nearly all of the recipes in this chapter contain whole wheat. Whole wheat not only boosts the nutritional value of these snacks, but also adds depth of flavor. Whole wheat has a nutty flavor that complements the roasted baked goods—perfect in the cracker recipes. White whole wheat flour is milder than whole wheat flour, both in texture and in flavor, and can be found in most grocery stores. So, let's preheat the oven and get baking!

## ingredients

- ~ 2½ cups (300 g) unbleached all-purpose flour
- ~ 1¼ cups (150 g) white whole wheat flour
- ~ 2 teaspoons salt
- ~ 2 teaspoons baking soda
- ~ 1½ cups (355 ml) buttermilk, plus ¼ cup (60 ml) for brushing*

## tools needed

- ~ measuring cups and spoons
- ~ liquid measuring cup
- ~ large mixing bowl
- ~ rimmed baking sheet
- ~ parchment paper
- ~ whisk
- ~ wooden spoon
- ~ serrated knife
- ~ pastry brush

*Who always has buttermilk on hand? Not me!
See page 27 for buttermilk substitutions.*

# Hearty
# SODA BREAD

This recipe is a great introduction to bread. It's a one-bowl recipe, easy to prepare, and takes under an hour to make from start to finish.

Yield: 1 loaf

Soda bread is hearty, delicious as toast for breakfast, and great for sopping up sauces from stews and soups. Don't expect this bread to have the same texture as yeast-leavened sandwich breads. To add extra flavor and a personal touch, let kids mix in nuts, seeds, or raisins from the pantry.

- Sunflower seeds, caraway seeds, poppy seeds, sesame seeds, pumpkin seeds, for sprinkling on top or mixing in.
- Raisins or dried cranberries for mixing in.

Add these ingredients to the dry ingredients before adding the buttermilk and/or sprinkle on top of the loaf just before baking.

A

# INSTRUCTIONS

1 Preheat the oven to 450°F (230°C, or gas mark 8). Line a baking sheet with parchment paper and set aside.

2 In a large mixing bowl, whisk together the flours, salt, and baking soda.

3 Place a fist into the middle of the flour mixture and move it in a small circle to create a well. (A) Pour in the 1½ cups (355 ml) buttermilk and mix with a spoon until the dough comes together into a ball.

*Make a well in the flour with your fist.*

Form the dough
into a loaf with
your hands.

4 Turn the dough out onto a
floured surface and knead
a few times just to bring
the dough together. (B) The
dough should feel tacky and
soft, but shouldn't come off
and stick to your hands. If
this happens, wash and dry
your hands and dust a little
bit of flour on them before
shaping the dough.

*To score the bread, cut about two-thirds of the way down into the loaf.*

## for smaller hands

Have younger kids help mix the dough with a spoon. Step in to turn out onto the floured surface and adjust the flour as needed, adding a bit more flour if the dough is too sticky to handle. To manage the mess, have your child shape the dough once it is no longer sticky. ∼

5 Shape the dough into a round loaf and place on the prepared baking sheet. Use a serrated knife to score the top of the bread with an X. (C) Be sure to extend the scores two-thirds of the way down into the bread. Using a pastry brush, brush the entire loaf with the remaining ¼ cup (60 ml) buttermilk.

## for smaller hands

Explain that brushing food is a lot like painting. You don't want too much paint on your brush, and it is the same for food. You are looking for an even coating of buttermilk on the loaf. ∼

6 Place the loaf in the oven on a middle rack for 15 minutes, then lower the temperature to 400°F (200°C, or gas mark 6) and rotate the pan. Bake for another 25 to 30 minutes, or until the crust is a deep, golden brown and sounds hollow when you tap the bottom of the loaf. Allow to cool for 20 to 30 minutes before slicing and serving.

## ingredients

- 3⅓ cups (400 g) unbleached all-purpose flour
- 2 cups (240 g) white whole wheat flour
- 2½ teaspoons salt
- 1 packet active dry yeast (or 2¼ teaspoons)
- 2 cups (470 ml) lukewarm water
- canola oil or any neutral-flavored oil

## *Easy Overnight* FRENCH BAGUETTES

**Start with the simple ingredients of flour, water, salt, and yeast, and watch their incredible transformation.**

Yield: **3** baguettes

## tools needed

~ measuring cups and spoons
~ liquid measuring cup
~ large mixing bowl
~ wooden spoon
~ rubber spatula
~ pastry brush
~ plastic wrap
~ bench scraper
~ dish towel or cheesecloth
~ baking stone or extra rimmed baking sheet
~ rimmed baking sheet or roasting pan
~ serrated knife

These baguettes fill your home with a wonderful scent and taste delicious. Start this bread with your kids after dinner on a Friday or Saturday night and have freshly baked bread ready by lunchtime the next day.

Mix the ingredients together.

# INSTRUCTIONS

1 *The night before you'd like to bake the bread,* combine the flours, salt, yeast, and water in a large mixing bowl and mix until combined and smooth. (A) Let rest, uncovered, for 5 minutes.

2 Using a bowl scraper, transfer the dough to a lightly floured work surface and knead for about 2 minutes. (B) The dough should feel smooth, soft, and slightly tacky. If the dough is too sticky, add a small amount of flour and knead for another minute or so.

*Knead the dough to develop the gluten, which helps allow the dough to rise.*

C

*Brush a small amount of oil in the bowl to make it easier for the bread to rise and to prevent sticking.*

4 *The next day, 2 hours before you plan to bake,* remove the dough from the refrigerator. Lightly dust the work surface with flour and turn out the dough. Divide the dough into thirds using a bench scraper. (D) Gently press each piece of dough into a rectangle, with the long sides facing you.

5 Fold the edge closest to you into the middle. (E) Flip the dough around so that the other long side is facing you and repeat, folding the dough to the middle, overlapping the crease. Pinch the dough to seal the crease.

6 Turn the dough over and roll back and forth, tapering the ends to form a baguette that is about 15 inches (38 cm) long. (F) Repeat with the other pieces of dough. Place the loaves on a floured dish towel or cheesecloth, with about 5 inches (12.5 cm) in between each loaf. Scrunch the towels in between the loaves to separate them with walls. This will prevent the loaves from flattening and help them maintain a round appearance. Cover lightly with plastic wrap and allow to proof at room temperature for 1½ hours, or until the dough increases to 1½ times its original size.

7 About 45 minutes to an hour before baking, place a baking stone or an upside-down baking sheet on the middle to lower rack of your oven. Preheat the oven to 500°F (250°C, or gas mark 10) or as high as your oven will go. Place a rimmed baking sheet or roasting pan on the rack underneath.

### for smaller hands

Children can help brush the oil with a pastry brush. Before placing the dough in the bowl, double-check the bowl to ensure that they didn't miss any spots! ~

3 Wash and dry the bowl in which you mixed the dough, and brush a small amount of oil on the entire inside of the bowl. (C) Place the dough inside and cover the bowl with plastic wrap. Place the bowl in the refrigerator to chill overnight.

*Divide the dough into thirds.*

*Fold the edge closest to you into the middle.*

*Roll back and forth, tapering the ends to form a baguette.*

8 When you are ready to bake, score the baguettes diagonally across the top of the loaves with a serrated knife, cutting ½ inch (1.3 cm) into the loaves. Carefully transfer the dough to the preheated baking stone or upside-down baking sheet. Pour 1 cup (235 ml) of water into the baking sheet on the bottom rack of the oven. Lower the oven temperature to 450°F (230°C, or gas mark 8).

### for smaller hands

Have children watch steps 7 and 8 from a distance, as the knives are sharp and the oven is very hot. You need to move quickly to transfer the loaves to the hot oven and a child may get in the way of this step.  ~

### for smaller hands

Have children help seal the crease of the dough and roll out into a baguette shape. Because you do not want to deflate the dough, show them how to use a gentle yet firm touch when handling the dough.  ~

9 Bake for 25 to 30 minutes, rotating the pan halfway through. The baguettes are done when the crust is golden brown and the loaves sound hollow when you tap the bottom. You can also check for doneness by inserting a thermometer into the loaf to measure the internal temperature—it should be about 200°F (93°C).

10 Now for the most difficult part—you must wait until the bread is cool before slicing it—about 45 minutes.

## ingredients

**For Pretzels:**
- ~ 2 cups (470 ml) warm water
- ~ 2 tablespoons (30 ml) honey
- ~ 1 packet active dry yeast (or 2¼ teaspoons)
- ~ 2 cups (240 g) white whole wheat flour
- ~ 1 tablespoon (18 g) salt
- ~ 1 teaspoon dry mustard powder
- ~ 4 cups (480 g) unbleached all-purpose flour
- ~ 2 teaspoons vegetable oil or other neutral-flavored oil

**For Honey Mustard Glaze:**
- ~ 1 large egg yolk
- ~ 3 tablespoons (45 ml) honey
- ~ 1 tablespoon (11 g) Dijon mustard
- ~ 1 teaspoon dry mustard powder

- ~ coarse sea salt or pretzel salt

*Honey Mustard*
# SOFT PRETZELS

**These pretzels are very similar to the soft, delicious pretzels most commonly found in malls.**

*Yield:* **13** *pretzels*

## tools needed

~ measuring cups and spoons
~ liquid measuring cup
~ large mixing bowl
~ small bowl
~ wooden spoon
~ plastic wrap
~ 2 rimmed baking sheets
~ parchment paper
~ pastry brush

After countless recipe tests and happy recipe tasters, I've found that skipping the traditional step of simmering the pretzels in a baking soda bath before baking allowed the subtle honey mustard flavor to shine—and, best of all, it makes this snack project easier! Adults will enjoy these pretzels warm from the oven dipped in mustard, but younger palates may prefer a honey-sweetened mustard.

*Activate the yeast in the warm water.*

# INSTRUCTIONS

1 Pour the warm water and honey into a large mixing bowl. Sprinkle with the yeast, stir gently, and let sit for 10 minutes; the yeast should be foamy. (A)

### for smaller hands

Yeast is a fun science experiment for children. I like to explain to children in a silly way that yeast leavens our bread during downtime (even if it may not be in scientific terms). Yeast is a living thing, a fungus actually, and when it is dried up it is "asleep." We wake up the yeast in warm water, like a warm bath. When added to flour, the yeast gobbles up the flour because it's their favorite food. They create a gas (just like we burp!) and that creates air bubbles in our dough, which makes it a puff up and rise. The air bubbles in bread are the yeast's "burps"! Be prepared for yeast burp jokes and giggle fests. ~

**B**

While you knead, soak the mixing bowl to make cleanup easier!

*Mix the ingredients to form a shaggy dough. Stop adding flour once the dough is tacky.*

**C**

*Form a loop with the tails facing you.*

2 Add 1 cup (120 g) of the white whole wheat flour, the salt, and the dry mustard powder to the yeast mixture, mixing with a wooden spoon until combined. Add the remaining 1 cup (120 g) of the white whole wheat flour, and mix until combined. (B) Add the unbleached flour by the cup until the dough comes together in a ball and feels tacky. Resist the urge to add more flour—you want the dough to have just enough flour so you can begin kneading. Transfer the dough to a lightly floured surface, and soak the mixing bowl to make cleanup easier. Knead the dough for about 5 minutes, or until smooth and elastic. Wash your mixing bowl and wipe dry with a towel. Lightly oil the inside of the bowl.

3 Place the dough inside the oiled bowl, turning it to completely cover all sides with a thin film of oil. Cover bowl with plastic wrap, (I like to cover the bowl with a plate instead to save plastic), and leave in a warm spot for 1 hour, or until dough has doubled in size.

### for smaller hands

Cut the dough into pieces and give a piece to each child to knead, so that everyone gets a chance to play with the dough. Smaller pieces are easier to knead with small hands than the whole ball of dough. Place a bowl of flour for children to dip their hands into when the dough starts feeling too sticky for them. ~

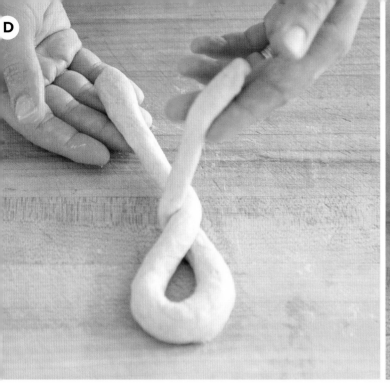

*Twist the center twice around.*

*Bring the loop toward you, folding it over the tails.*

4 Preheat the oven to 450°F (230°C, or gas mark 8). Line 2 baking sheets with parchment paper and set aside. Punch down the dough and transfer to a lightly floured cutting board. Knead once or twice and divide into 13 pieces (about 2½ ounces [70 g] each if you are using a scale to measure).

### for smaller hands

Children can help cut the dough in this step using a bench scraper. Cut one piece of dough as an example and place near children to they can match their dough pieces to the example. Encourage them to use the example piece to decide whether the dough is too big or too small instead of asking you. This approach gives them the independence to decide for themselves, resulting in a sense of confidence. ~

5 Wipe off excess flour from your work surface. You want to have some surface tension to roll out your dough, and more flour will make your dough slip around. Roll each piece of dough into a strip 18 inches (45.7 cm) long. Twist into a pretzel shape (see photos C–E for instruction), and transfer to the prepared baking sheets. Cover with a kitchen towel and continue to form pretzels. You want to leave about 2 inches (5 cm) of space between each pretzel. Let the pretzels rest until they rise slightly, about 15 minutes.

Children often have difficulty forming the dough balls into ropes. Make it easier by starting the rope for them and having them finish it. You may have to show them the pretzel-forming process several times before they understand!  ~

6 For the honey mustard glaze, combine all the ingredients in a small bowl until the mixture is smooth. Brush the pretzels evenly with the glaze using a pastry brush. Sprinkle with salt. (F)

7 Bake for 12 to 15 minutes, or until golden brown. Let cool on a wire rack for at least 15 minutes. Pretzels are best when eaten the same day, but they will keep at room temperature, uncovered, for up to 2 days. Do not store in a covered container or they will become soggy.

# Honey Mustard
# DIPPING SAUCE

**This sauce is a classic accompaniment to the pretzels.**

### ingredients

~ ¼ cup (60 ml) honey
~ 2 tablespoons (22 g) Dijon mustard

### tools needed

~ measuring cups and spoons
~ small mixing bowl
~ whisk or fork

*Yield: Generous ¼ cup (60 ml), enough for* **5** *pretzels*

1 In a small bowl, mix together the honey and mustard thoroughly. Check for seasoning—different mustards have different levels of spice. For younger palates, add more honey to balance the spiciness of the mustard.

Brush the pretzels with the glaze and sprinkle each with salt.

## ingredients

- ~ 1 cup (235 ml) water
- ~ 1 stick (½ cup, or 112 g) unsalted butter
- ~ 2 teaspoons salt
- ~ 1 teaspoon sugar
- ~ 1 cup (120 g) unbleached all-purpose flour
- ~ 1½ cups (180 g) grated sharp Cheddar cheese, plus ¼ cup (30 g) for sprinkling
- ~ ¼ cup (25 g) finely grated Parmesan cheese
- ~ ¼ teaspoon paprika
- ~ 5 large eggs

**For Egg Wash:**
- ~ 1 large egg
- ~ 1 tablespoon (15 ml) water

## *Fancy-Schmancy Cheesy*
# CHEDDAR PUFFS

Not your average cheese puff, these snacks are delicious as well as elegant. The fancy term for this French pastry is *pâte à choux*. You can make the dough without the cheese and paprika and use it as a base for éclairs and cream puffs. Have your kids help out with your next dinner party using this easy and savory recipe!

*Yield: about* **50** *cheese puf*

## tools needed

measuring cups and spoons
large mixing bowl
small mixing bowl
cheese grater
2 rimmed baking sheets
parchment paper
heavy-bottomed pot
wooden spoon
pastry bag and ½-inch (1.3 cm) pastry tip
pastry brush

*Cooked ingredients,
ready to remove
from the heat.*

# INSTRUCTIONS

1 Preheat the oven to 375°F (190°C, or gas mark 5). Line 2 baking sheets with parchment paper and set aside.

### for smaller hands

Children can help grate cheese only if they understand that graters are not toys and they can cut you if you are not careful. Cheese-grating accidents are reduced greatly when the child slowly grates the cheese, making sure to hand off the piece of cheese once it gets too small to grate safely. When handling grated cheese, sometimes kids get excited and want to squish the cheese. Show your child how to sprinkle the cheese all over so that it doesn't clump together. ~

### for smaller hands

For this recipe, small children may watch as you complete the steps involving the stove. Have children help measure ingredients and grate cheese, and then they can stand on a stool to watch you stir the ingredients on the stove. ~

2 In a medium saucepan, combine the water, butter, salt, and sugar over medium-high heat. Bring the mixture to a boil, and immediately remove from the heat. Using a wooden spoon, add the flour, stirring continuously, until the mixture is combined. Return the pan to medium-high heat. Cook, stirring constantly, until the mixture pulls away from the sides of the pan and forms a film on the bottom, about 5 minutes. (A)

3 Remove the mixture from the heat and transfer the dough to a medium-size mixing bowl. Add the 1½ cups (180 g) Cheddar, the Parmesan, and the paprika. Stir to combine with a wooden spoon and let cool slightly, 3 to 5 minutes.

## for smaller hands

Children can add the eggs, one at a time, if the eggs are separated into small bowls. Mixing the eggs by hand can prove to be difficult, even for adults, so mix until the egg is almost incorporated and hand over the bowl to the child for a last mix before adding more eggs. ~

4 Add the eggs, one at a time, stirring vigorously after each addition, and wait to add the next egg until the previous one is entirely incorporated. (B)

5 For the egg wash, whisk together the egg and water in a small bowl.

6 Transfer the dough to a pastry bag fitted with a ½-inch (1.3 cm) round tip (C) and pipe 1½-inch (3.8 cm) puffs about 1 inch (2.5 cm) apart on your baking sheet. (D) Brush each puff with the egg wash and sprinkle each one with remaining ¼ cup (30 g) Cheddar cheese. (E) Alternatively, you can use two spoons to portion each cheese puff (see page 23).

Add the eggs one at a time.

**B**

*Handy tip: Prop the piping bag in a measuring cup or other container.*

*Pipe the batter onto the baking sheet in a circular motion.*

*Sprinkle cheese onto each cheese puff.*

7 Bake, rotating the baking sheets halfway through, until the puffs are golden, 20 to 25 minutes. Pull the cheese puffs from the oven slowly, as they can deflate. Test a cheese puff for doneness by breaking it open. If a lot of steam escapes, bake for a few minutes more. A properly cooked cheese puff is hollow on the inside with a small amount of moisture and lightly crispy on the outside. Serve immediately, as cheese puffs are most delicious when eaten warm from the oven.

### for smaller hands

You can show your child how to make even-size cheese puffs, but brushing with egg and sprinkling with cheese may be a more fun option. It is important that each puff is roughly the same size to ensure even cooking. ~

## ingredients

- ~ ¾ cup (90 g) white whole wheat flour
- ~ ⅛ teaspoon garlic powder
- ~ ¼ teaspoon salt, plus more for sprinkling
- ~ 4 tablespoons (56 g) unsalted butter, cut into small cubes and chilled
- ~ 1½ cups (180 g) coarsely grated sharp Cheddar cheese
- ~ 1 to 2 tablespoons (15 to 30 ml) cold milk

# CHEDDAR SQUARES

The amazing thing about homemade versions of brand-name snacks is that their flavor is incredible and the ingredient list is a fraction of the size.

*Yield: about*  *cracker*

## tools needed

~ measuring cups and spoons
~ medium-size mixing bowl
~ cheese grater
~ whisk
~ pastry cutter
~ wooden spoon
~ plastic wrap
~ 2 baking sheets
~ parchment paper
~ wooden cutting boards
~ rolling pin
~ pizza cutter
~ bamboo skewer
~ bench scraper

It's important to use high-quality butter and cheese when making this recipe, as they constitute the majority of the ingredients! Feel free to use your favorite semi-hard cheese instead. I imagine Gruyère would add a special touch to these crackers.

### for smaller hands

Measuring is very fun for small children—and you'd be surprised how seriously they take it, especially if you show them the proper way to do it (see proper measuring techniques on page 20). ~

# INSTRUCTIONS

1  Preheat the oven to 350°F (180°C, or gas mark 4).

2  In a medium-size mixing bowl, whisk together the flour, garlic powder, and salt.

3  Gently toss the butter cubes and cheese into the flour mixture. (A) Using a pastry cutter, cut the butter and cheese into the flour. The end result should look like wet sand with some distinguishable butter and Cheddar pieces scattered throughout the dough. Be careful not to overmix, or the crackers will be tough.

*Cut the butter and cheese into the flour using your fingertips.*

*Pour in the milk, 1 tablespoon (15 ml) at a time.*

*Set up your workstations before getting started. Make sure you have cookie cutters, flour, and your baking sheet handy.*

4 Add 1 tablespoon (15 ml) of milk at a time, using a spoon to mix it in. (B) The dough should be just moist enough to stick together when you form it into a ball. The dough will seem very crumbly, but the cheese will hold it together—just knead it a few times to incorporate any stray crumbs. Wrap the dough in plastic wrap and chill in the fridge for 15 to 20 minutes.

5 Set up your workstations. (C) Line 2 baking sheets with parchment paper. Each person making crackers will need a wooden cutting board (working at the kitchen table with a plastic mat also works), a small bowl of flour, a rolling pin, a bamboo skewer, cookie cutters, and a bench scraper. Lightly flour your work surface. Working with pieces the size of a golf ball, roll out each dough ball to about ⅛ inch (3 mm) thick, turning to maintain a square shape. (D) If the dough sticks at all to the surface, use a bench scraper to loosen it.

### for smaller hands

Rolling out cracker dough may be difficult for small children. Instead, reserve a piece of dough from the batch and let them play with it like play dough while you roll out your first batch of dough. ~

Roll out the dough; it may be a little crumbly.

E

*Use cookie cutters to cut out cracker shapes.*

## Do-Ahead Tip

Cracker dough freezes well when wrapped in plastic wrap. To store the dough in the freezer for later use, cut the dough in half and shape into flat squares before wrapping twice in plastic wrap. On baking day, thaw the dough for a couple of hours and proceed with the recipe.

F

*Poke a hole using the blunt end of a skewer.*

**6** Using your bench scraper or a pizza cutter, make a grid on your cracker dough and cut into 1½-inch (3.8 cm) squares. Gently push the scrap pieces to the side of your workspace and reserve. Lift the crackers with the bench scraper or an offset spatula and place on your baking sheets. Poke a hole in the center of each cracker with the blunt end of a bamboo skewer. (F) It is okay if some of the crackers are touching. Sprinkle the crackers with a small amount of salt before placing them in the oven.

### for smaller hands

While cutting the crackers into squares is more efficient, kids can help cut crackers using bite-size cookie cutters. (E) Kids have a natural inclination to put their cookie cutter right in the middle of the dough—instead, show them how to work from the edges and use all the dough. Play a game to see how many crackers you can fit in the rolled-out dough. You can combine the scraps and reroll to make more crackers. This is also a great opportunity to practice counting! ~

**7** Bake the crackers for 12 to 15 minutes, rotating the pans halfway through and alternating racks. The crackers are done when the edges and bottom are golden brown. Remove from the oven and set the baking sheets on a rack to cool. These crackers will keep in a tightly covered container for a few days —if they make it that long before being devoured!

## ingredients

- ~ 2 cups (240 g) unbleached all-purpose flour
- ~ 1 cup (120 g) white whole wheat flour
- ~ 1 teaspoon salt, plus more for sprinkling
- ~ 1 cup (235 ml) warm water
- ~ ⅓ cup (80 ml) extra-virgin olive oil, plus more for coating and brushing

# *Crispy Crunchy* OLIVE OIL CRACKERS

These crackers are very simple to prepare and the dough is forgiving—you can collect the scraps left over from cutting the crackers several times to make more crackers. These crackers are delicious on their own, dipped into hummus, or sprinkled over soup!

*Yield: about*  **150** *crackers*

## tools needed

~ measuring cups and spoons
~ liquid measuring cup
~ large mixing bowl
~ whisk
~ wooden spoon
~ plastic wrap
~ baking sheets
~ parchment paper
~ rolling pin
~ assortment of cookie cutters
  (optional, but more fun)
~ pizza cutter
~ bench scraper
~ bamboo skewer or fork

*Mix the ingredients together
until they form a ball of dough.*

# INSTRUCTIONS

**1** In a large mixing bowl, whisk together the flours
and salt.

**2** Add the water and olive oil. Mix with a wooden
spoon until the dough forms a ball. (A)

### for smaller hands

This recipe is a great starter recipe for children, as
it's easy enough to make from start to finish. I have
taught children as young as four to mix the dough in
teams of two. The challenge in this recipe is making
sure the dough is rolled out thin enough, which is
where an adult can step in to help out.  ~

### for smaller hands

Have children measure and mix the dough in steps
1 and 2. Form the dough into a ball and add flour
as needed to make it a manageable consistency for
kneading. Cut the dough into pieces and give a piece
to each child to knead, so that everyone has a chance
to play with the dough. Smaller pieces are easier to
knead with small hands than the whole ball of dough.
Place a bowl of flour for children to dip their hands
into when the dough starts feeling too sticky for
them. This prevents children from adding too much
flour too often, which results in tough, dry dough.  ~

*Knead the dough. You can split the dough and give a piece to each child.*

C

Use a
rolling pin to
roll out the
dough.

Older children are able to roll out
the dough thin enough for the
recipe. Younger children have more
fun cutting the dough. That being
said, do let young children have a
hand in rolling out the dough, or at
least rolling it out as thin as they
can before passing it off to an adult.
~

3   Gather up all the leftover crumbs
and dough and transfer to a lightly
floured surface. Knead the dough
until smooth, about 5 minutes. (B)

4   Lightly coat the ball of dough in
olive oil and wrap in plastic wrap.
Allow the dough to rest for
30 minutes.

5   Preheat the oven to 450°F (230°C,
or gas mark 8). Line baking sheets
with parchment paper.

6   Working with one-fourth of the
dough at a time, use a rolling pin
to roll out the dough until it is
about ⅛ inch (3 mm) thick. (C)

BREADS AND SNACKS

91

*With adult supervision, use a pizza cutter to cut the crackers.*

7 Using cookie cutters or a pizza cutter, cut out desired cracker shapes. (D) If cutting using a pizza cutter, cut squares into 2-inch (5 cm) pieces. If you would like larger or smaller crackers, adjust the baking times accordingly. Place the crackers on the prepared baking sheets, brush lightly with olive oil, and sprinkle with salt.

## for smaller hands

Have children help sprinkle the finishing salt over the crackers. When sprinkling finishing salt on baked goods, hold your hand high above the item you are seasoning. This helps disperse the salt evenly, so you don't have one cracker loaded with salt and another that has no seasoning. Children tend to go overboard on the salt, but it's because they don't understand why they shouldn't. Explain that overly salted food is inedible.  ~

8 Using a bamboo skewer or toothpick, poke a few holes in each cracker to allow steam to escape.

## for smaller hands

Poking holes in the crackers is fun for kids. To avoid crackers with more holes than cracker, give kids a number to work with for each cracker. Two to five holes per cracker is a good range.  ~

9 Bake for 10 to 12 minutes, or until lightly golden on the edges. Allow to cool completely on a cooling rack. The crackers will become crisp as they cool.

Add fresh herbs for savory herb crackers.

## Flavored Variations

### Savory Herb Crackers

Add in about 1 tablespoon of a mix of your favorite chopped herbs, such as rosemary, thyme, sage, and parsley. For a different flavor, minced tarragon and chives are also delicious.

### Fuschia Crackers

Boil 3 beets until tender. Peel and puree the beets in a small food processor or blender, adding a small amount of water if needed. Add the beet puree to the water before mixing in with the flour. You may need to add a little extra flour if the dough is too sticky. While the beet flavor will be subtle, it will lend a slight sweetness as well as vibrant fuchsia color!

*Add beet puree to the water and oil mixture to make fuchsia-colored crackers.*

## ingredients

- ~ 1¼ cups (150 g) white whole wheat flour
- ~ ½ cup (120 g) lightly packed golden brown sugar
- ~ ½ teaspoon baking soda
- ~ ½ teaspoon salt
- ~ 4 tablespoons (56 g) unsalted butter, cut into small cubes and chilled
- ~ 3 tablespoons (45 ml) honey
- ~ 3 tablespoons (45 ml) whole milk
- ~ 2 teaspoons pure vanilla extract

**For Cinnamon Sugar Topping:**
- ~ 3 tablespoons (36 g) granulated sugar
- ~ 1½ teaspoons ground cinnamon

*Good-for-You*
# GRAHAM CRACKERS

When comparing store-bought to homemade, these graham crackers hit a home run in the flavor department. They are excellent for snacking with a glass of cold milk and delectable in campfire s'mores.

*Yield: about* **25** *crackers*

## tools needed

- ~ measuring cups and spoons
- ~ liquid measuring cup
- ~ large mixing bowl
- ~ small mixing bowl
- ~ whisk
- ~ plastic wrap
- ~ bench scraper
- ~ wooden spoon
- ~ jar with lid
- ~ rolling pin
- ~ pizza cutter
- ~ assorted cookie cutters (optional, but more fun)
- ~ bamboo skewer
- ~ baking sheets
- ~ parchment paper

# INSTRUCTIONS

**1** Combine the flour, brown sugar, baking soda, and salt in a large mixing bowl. Mix with a whisk until combined. Add the butter and toss to coat in the flour mixture. (A) Cut the butter into the flour until it takes on the appearance of wet sand with some visible chunks of butter.

*Before adding the liquid ingredients, the mixture should look like wet sand.*

**2** In a separate bowl, whisk together the honey, milk, and vanilla. (B) Add to the flour mixture and mix until just combined. The dough will be very soft. Lay out a large piece of plastic wrap and dust it lightly with flour, then turn the dough out onto it and pat it into a rectangle. Wrap it completely, then chill until firm, about 2 hours or overnight.

*Whisk together the liquid ingredients.*

**3** Meanwhile, for the topping, place the ingredients in a small jar and shake to combine. (C)

### for smaller hands

This is a great step for children to take ownership on; just make sure that if it is a glass jar they don't drop it while shaking! ∼

**4** Once the dough has been chilled, divide it in half and return one half to the refrigerator. Lightly flour your work surface and roll out the dough about ⅛ inch (3 mm) thick. (D) You may want to have extra flour and a bench scraper handy in case the dough begins to stick. (E)

**5** Using a bench scraper or a pizza cutter, cut the crackers into 2½-inch (6.4 cm) squares. (F)

**6** Adjust the oven racks to the upper and lower positions and preheat the oven to 350°F (180°C, or gas mark 4). Line baking sheets with parchment paper.

### for smaller hands

Make an example cracker for children to refer to when they are poking the holes. Part of the cuteness of these crackers is that they have similar markings, so explain to your child that the goal is to make each cracker look the same! ∼

*Use a jar to mix together cinnamon and sugar. A bowl also works.*

*Since the dough is on the sticky side, sprinkle with some flour before rolling out.*

*Use a bench scraper to lift the sticky dough.*

**C**

**D**

**E**

**F**

*Cut the dough into squares using a bench scraper.*

**G**

Graham crackers ready for the oven!

### for smaller hands

Because the dough is quite sticky to begin with, have children help by cutting the dough into crackers after you have already rolled it out. ~

7 Place the crackers on the prepared baking sheets and sprinkle with the cinnamon sugar topping. Poke 6 holes (2 lines of 3) in each of the crackers using the blunt side of a wooden skewer. (G) Repeat with the second batch of dough (or freeze for later use). Finally, gather any scraps together into a ball, chill until firm, and reroll.

### for smaller hands

Have children help sprinkle the cinnamon sugar over the crackers. If children get overzealous with salt, you can bet that they will have the same if not more enthusiasm with sugar. When sprinkling finishing sugar on baked goods, hold your hand high above the item you are seasoning. This helps disperse the mixture evenly. ~

8 Check the crackers after 10 minutes and rotate the sheets. Bake for another 2 minutes if necessary. The crackers are done when they have browned and are slightly firm to the touch. They will continue to crisp as they cool.

Chapter 6

# Delicious DESSERTS

## recipe box

"Impress Your Grandma"
Pie Crust

Mini Hand Pies

Homemade Whipped Cream

Flourless Milk Chocolate
Cake

Easy-Peasy
Mini Cheesecakes

# EVERYONE LOVES DESSERT!

**There is something satisfying to ending a meal with a sweet treat. In this chapter you will find a dessert for everyone. There are chocolaty desserts, cold desserts, and warm, fruity desserts.**

Many of these desserts can be made ahead of time or at least parts can be made in advance to reduce the stress of making a multistep recipe all at once. For instance, you can prepare the pie crust (page 100) for mini hand pies a week before you plan to make the pies, as the crust can be easily frozen. With a little advance planning, you can include the kids in fun and engaging way.

## Looking for a Gluten-Free Dessert?

Although there are not many recipes in this book to accommodate this dietary restriction, there are a few recipes in this chapter that are either naturally gluten free or can be made gluten free quite easily. Make the flourless chocolate cake or cheesecakes minus the graham cracker crust. Another idea is to prepare the pie filling of macerated fruit and serve with a dollop of whipped cream. That way you can make a dessert without having your gluten-free guest feel left out, especially if that gluten-free guest is a child.

## ingredients

- ¾ cup (90 g) all-purpose flour
- ¼ cup (30 g) white whole wheat flour
- ½ teaspoon salt
- 1 stick (½ cup, or 112 g) cold unsalted butter
- 3 tablespoons (45 ml) ice water, or as needed

## tools needed

- measuring cups and spoons
- liquid measuring cup
- medium mixing bowl
- whisk
- bench scraper
- wooden spoon
- pastry cutter or 2 butter knives
- plastic wrap
- rolling pin

## "Impress Your Grandma"
# PIE CRUST

In my family, Grandma is the queen of pie crusts. Her pies are always flaky, never tough. What's her secret? My sister and I called it "grandma hands," because she is such a gentle person and always handles the dough so delicately.

*Yield: enough dough for* **4-5** *mini hand pies or* **1** *9-inch (23 cm) single pie crust*

I try to channel my grandmother's approach when making this recipe, taking care to not overmix the dough. Although her recipe included canola oil, I prefer an all-butter crust for flavor, as well as the addition of some whole wheat flour for extra nutrients. For a flaky pie crust, make sure all the ingredients are very cold. This crust is very versatile and can be used for sweet and savory applications, including the mini hand pies later in this chapter, quiches, and pot pies. Although I have never made this pie crust for my grandmother, I think she would be impressed.

# INSTRUCTIONS

1 In a medium mixing bowl, whisk together the flours and salt. Set aside.

2 Using a bench scraper, cut the butter into pea-size pieces (A) and place on a plate; chill in the freezer for 5 minutes.

3 Fill a liquid measuring cup with cold water and place an ice cube in it. Set aside.

*Cut the butter into cubes using a bench scraper.*

### for smaller hands

This is a handy trick that I learned from a fellow cook while I was working in a restaurant. To avoid handling the butter and warming it, use your bench scraper to cut up the butter. Show children how to make the same size cubes by cutting the butter into 4 slices lengthwise. Then stack the slices on top of each other and make 4 more slices lengthwise, turning the slices into strips. Stack the sticks to make the shape of a stick of butter, and then slice across the stick to form cubes. It is more important that the pieces of butter are a consistent size, even if they are not quite the size of peas. ~

*Toss the butter with flour.*

*Use your fingertips to pinch the flour into the butter.*

*The dough is ready to add water.*

4 Once your butter is very cold, add it to your flour mixture and gently toss (B) with a wooden spoon or clean hands. If some butter pieces are still clinging together, gently break them up with your fingers (C) as you sprinkle the butter into the flour.

![hand] **for smaller hands**

There is no need to smash the butter into the flour at this point. Show your child how to toss the flour to make sure that each cube is coated before proceeding to the next step. ~

5 Use a pastry cutter, 2 butter knives, or light fingertips to cut the butter into the flour until the mixture looks like wet sand with some visible pieces of butter scattered throughout. Do not overmix. (D)

6 Add the ice water to the flour mixture 1 tablespoon (15 ml) at a time, and stir with a spoon. Once you have added 2 tablespoons (30 ml), try to smash the dough into a ball. (E) If the dough sticks together, then there is enough water. If the dough is still crumbly and doesn't hold together, then add more water. Once the dough adheres together, spread a sheet of plastic wrap on your work surface. Turn the dough onto the plastic, (F) wrap tightly, and chill for at least 1 hour or until ready to use.

## for smaller hands

Explain to children that you will not necessarily need all the water, but you place it in a cup to chill it with an ice cube. Having it in a cup makes it easier to measure 1 tablespoon (15 ml) at a time. Many times during my cooking classes I've had children dump in all the water in the cup, and it makes their dough goopy and hard to handle. ~

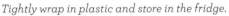

*Tightly wrap in plastic and store in the fridge.*

Gather up the dough in a ball.

E

F

103

## ingredients

**For Filling:**
- ~ 1 cup (145 g) strawberries or other berry, diced into ½-inch (1.3 cm) cubes
- ~ zest of 1 lemon
- ~ 1 tablespoon (12 g) sugar

**For Egg Wash:**
- ~ 1 large egg
- ~ 1 tablespoon (15 ml) water

- ~ 1 "Impress Your Grandma" Pie Crust (page 100), chilled
- ~ flour
- ~ sugar, for sprinkling

# MINI HAND PIES

In my opinion, these are much more fun to make than a large 9-inch (23 cm) pie crust. They don't take as long to bake, which is great if you are looking for a quick dessert. And it can be even quicker if you make the dough ahead of time and store it in the freezer!

*Yield:* **4-5** *personal-size pie*

## tools needed

measuring cups and spoons
2 small mixing bowls
Microplane zester
wooden spoon
fork or whisk
rolling pin
bench scraper
baking sheet
parchment paper
canning jar ring or round cookie
cutter measuring about 3½ inches
(9 cm) in diameter
pastry brush
sharp paring knife

The filling is for spring and summer berries, but feel free to swap in diced apples or pears, or even some spiced pumpkin puree mixed with ricotta cheese for a warming fall treat. If you would like to use frozen fruit, allow it to thaw first and drain any excess liquid before proceeding with the recipe.

*Cut strawberries for the filling.*

# INSTRUCTIONS

**1** Preheat the oven to 350°F (180°C, or gas mark 4).

### for smaller hands

Children can easily slice strawberries with a butter knife. Berries like blackberries, raspberries, and blueberries can be left whole. Make sure your child zests the lemon slowly to prevent accidents! ~

## What is Macerating?

Macerating is when you add sugar to cut fruit in order to draw out some of the juices, making the fruit a little bit saucy. Try topping ice cream with macerated fruit for a healthier alternative to flavored syrups.

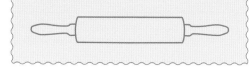

2 For the filling, mix all the ingredients in a small bowl and macerate (soften) for 5 minutes. (A)

3 For the egg wash, use a fork or whisk to mix together the egg wash ingredients in a small bowl and set aside.

4 Before rolling out your pie crust, generously flour your work surface. Wooden countertops or a large cutting board are great places to roll out your pie crust, but any clean and smooth work surface will do. Rub the rolling pin with a small amount of flour as well.

Mix the filling ingredients together.

## for smaller hands

Show children how to flour the work surface. For this recipe you actually want a decent bit of flour spread evenly on the work surface. Demonstrate how to sprinkle a handful of flour and spread it around with your hands. Make sure that they aren't just making a pile of flour. ~

**5** Using your rolling pin, flatten the dough until it is about ⅛ inch (3 mm) thick. (B) Try to keep the dough in a circle by turning the dough a quarter turn each time you roll the rolling pin back and forth. If the dough starts to stick to the work surface, use a bench scraper to gently loosen it. Add a small amount of flour as needed to prevent the dough from sticking.

**6** Line a baking sheet with parchment paper, place nearby, and begin to cut out your hand pies. Cut out the circles using a wide-mouth canning jar ring and place on the baking sheet. (C) If the dough circles begin to get too warm, place them in the fridge or freezer for a few minutes. Gather up any scraps and reroll the dough. You should be able to make 8 to 10 circles with all the dough. Take half of the dough circles and gently roll out slightly thinner and wider than the other half of the circles, about 4½ inches (11.5 cm) in diameter. You will use these as the tops of the pies. (Roll them out thinner to make sure the tops are large enough to cover the mound of filling.)

## for smaller hands

Cut the dough in half for children. It is easier to roll out smaller amounts of dough to start. ~

*Egg wash helps seal the edges together.*

*Spoon the filling onto the bottom crust.*

### for smaller hands

To avoid overworking the dough, try this game. Children often start using cookie cutters in the smack-dab middle of the dough and you end up only being able to fit in a few circles before you have to gather all the scraps and reroll it. Instead, try to see how many circles they can fit in the dough before they begin cutting. They can use the cutter to make small dents in the surface of the dough to show you how many they can fit. For really young children this is also a great opportunity to practice counting. ~

7 Once you are ready to begin assembling the pies, gather your egg wash and filling. Use a pastry brush to apply a small amount of egg wash on the outside rim of the dough. (D) Place 2 tablespoons (30 g) of filling in the center and top with the larger piece of dough. (E) Gently press around the sides of the filling to allow any air to escape and press around the edges to seal. (F) Press the edges with the tines of a fork to reinforce the seal and make a pretty pattern. Repeat with the remaining dough.

Ready for the oven.

*Place the top over the filling and gently press the edges to seal. Use a fork to press gently on the edges.*

### for smaller hands

Have children spoon the filling and use the fork to seal the edges. Make sure they do not use too much force and press all the way through with the fork.  ~

8 Brush the tops of the pies with egg wash and sprinkle with sugar. (G) Using a sharp paring knife, make 5 small air vents to allow the steam from the fruit to escape while baking. Chill the assembled pies in the fridge for 10 minutes before placing in the oven.

9 Bake the pies for 15 to 20 minutes, or until the tops and bottom are an even golden brown. Because the fruit filling is saucy, be sure to cook until golden brown to ensure that the pie crust isn't soggy. Serve warm with a dollop of whipped cream (page 110)!

### for smaller hands

Have children brush the pies with egg wash. Make sure they allow the egg to drip off the brush into the bowl to avoid putting too much egg wash on the pies. Children can sprinkle the sugar, but make sure they are sprinkling from a few feet above the pies to distribute the sugar evenly.  ~

## ingredients

~ ¼ cup (60 ml) heavy whipping cream
~ 1 teaspoon sugar
~ ¼ teaspoon pure vanilla extract

## tools needed

~ measuring spoons
~ liquid measuring cup
~ medium mixing bowl
~ whisk
~ rubber spatula

*Homemade*
# WHIPPED CREAM

Homemade whipped cream is heavenly, lightly sweetened, and one recipe where the flavor is by far superior to its store-bought equivalent in a can. Additionally, it takes almost no time to "whip up."

*Yield:* **4** *servings*

# INSTRUCTIONS

1  Place all the ingredients in a mixing bowl and whisk. Start slowly to prevent splashing, and once the cream thickens you can begin to whisk vigorously. Chilling the bowl and whisk ahead of time helps speed the whipping process.

### for smaller hands

Whisking whipped cream can go from a chore to a fun and friendly competition between siblings. Divide the cream between two bowls and have each child whisk to soft peaks. ~

2  Whisk the cream until it reaches soft peaks: When you lift the whisk, the cream retains its shape and doesn't drip off.

Whipped cream that has reached soft peaks.

## ingredients

- ~ 1½ sticks (¾ cup, or 168 g) unsalted butter (reserve the butter wrapper for greasing the pan)
- ~ 2 cups (350 g) high-quality milk chocolate disks or chopped milk chocolate
- ~ 6 eggs
- ~ ¼ cup (50 g) sugar
- ~ 2 teaspoons pure vanilla extract

# *Flourless*
# MILK CHOCOLATE CAKE

This cake is a delicious, creamy, gluten-free dessert option. The fluffy texture comes from properly whipped egg whites, so don't skimp on that step.

*Yield:*  **8-10** *servings*

## tools needed

- measuring cups and spoons
- 9-inch (23 cm) springform pan
- medium saucepan or soup pot
- 3 medium bowls, including one that fits inside the medium pot
- bench scraper
- whisk
- rubber spatula

When you pull this cake out of the oven, it will puff up and then deflate quickly—this is normal! This recipe requires several bowls, but if you only have two you can pour the melted chocolate and butter mixture into a small bowl to cool.

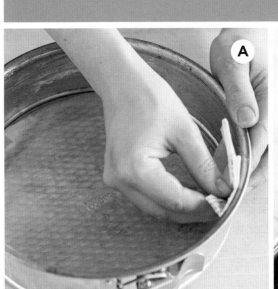

*Prepare the springform pan by greasing with butter paper.*

Double boiler setup.

# INSTRUCTIONS

**1** Preheat the oven to 350°F (180°C, or gas mark 4). Prepare the springform pan by greasing it with butter. (A)

### for smaller hands

Children can grease the pan with the butter wrapper, but check to make sure they don't miss any spots. ~

**2** Pour about 1 inch (2.5 cm) of water into the pot and place over medium heat. Add the butter and chocolate to the bowl that fits over the top of the pot. (B) Once the water begins to simmer, place the bowl on top and allow the butter and chocolate to gently melt. This technique is called a double boiler.

### for smaller hands

Have children cut the butter into cubes using a bench scraper. ~

*Whipping the egg whites adds a light texture to the cake.*

*Fold the egg whites into the batter gently.*

3 While the butter and chocolate are melting, separate the eggs, placing the whites in one bowl and the yolks in another. When the chocolate is about 75 percent melted, remove the mixture from the heat. The heat of the melted chocolate will melt the rest of the mixture. Mix until smooth and set aside.

### for smaller hands

Separate the eggs for children. It is very difficult to whip the egg whites when even the smallest amount of egg yolk gets into them. ~

4 Add 2 tablespoons (25 g) of the sugar each to the bowl of egg yolks and the bowl of egg whites. Whisk the yolks until they are pale yellow and have begun to thicken. Add the vanilla and mix to combine. Pour the chocolate mixture into the egg yolks and mix thoroughly.

### for smaller hands

Have children measure the sugar and pour it into each bowl. ~

**5** With a clean whisk, beat the egg whites until they form stiff peaks. (C) Gently mix one-third of the egg whites into the chocolate batter with a rubber spatula. (D) Fold in the remaining egg whites gently, taking care to preserve the air in the whites. For more about this technique, see page 25 in the techniques section.

### for smaller hands

As with making whipped cream (page 110), it helps to turn this job into a friendly competition, or simply take turns to avoid fatigue. You may even want to have a quick shoulder-stretching session prior to whisking the egg whites! ~

**6** Pour the batter into the prepared pan (E) and bake on the middle rack for 20 to 30 minutes, or until a toothpick or butter knife inserted into the center comes out with moist crumbs attached. (F) Begin checking for doneness at 20 minutes, checking every 3 minutes. It is important to not overbake this cake, as it will lose its creaminess. Serve with whipped cream (page 110).

*Using a rubber spatula, pour the batter into the pan.*

E

F

*Pull the cake from the oven when moist crumbs remain on the tester.*

## ingredients

**For Graham Cracker Crust:**

~ 1 cup (120 g) ground-up graham crackers (about ½ recipe of Good-for-You Graham Crackers, page 94, or thirteen 2½ × 2½-inch [6.5 × 6.5 cm] crackers)

~ 2 tablespoons (28 g) unsalted butter, melted

~ 1 tablespoon (12 g) sugar

**For Cheesecake Filling:**

~ 1 cup (230 g) cream cheese

~ ¼ cup (50 g) sugar

~ 1 large egg

~ ½ teaspoon pure vanilla extract

~ zest of 1 lemon (optional)

~ ⅓ cup (80 ml) cream or whole milk (or a combination of the two)

~ macerated fruit pie filling (page 104) or warm chocolate sauce (optional)

*Easy-Peasy*
# MINI CHEESECAKES

These delicious, small treats provide the perfect ending to a meal or dinner party. Light yet creamy, with a rich, crunchy crust, these cheesecakes are excellent topped with macerated fruit pie filling or warm chocolate sauce. If you have time, use the homemade graham crackers in the crust (page 94).

*Yield:* **9** *mini cheesecake*

## tools needed

~ measuring cups and spoons
~ small mixing bowls
~ Microplane zester
~ standard-size 12-cup muffin tin
~ paper muffin liners
~ wooden spoon
~ whisk
~ rubber scraper
~ roasting pan
~ teakettle or pitcher
~ plastic wrap

*Mix the crust ingredients together.*

### Grinding Crackers

To grind up graham crackers, use a small food processor, blender, or mortar and pestle. Keep in mind that you do not want the crumbs to be superfine; you want them to have some texture remaining. If you do not have a food processor, blender, or mortar and pestle, you can also use a mixing bowl and cutting board. Using about ¼ cup (30 g) at a time, crush a pile of graham cracker crumbles on a cutting board by rolling the side of the bowl across the crackers. Place the graham cracker crumbs in a bowl before working on the next ¼ cup (30 g) of crumbles.

# INSTRUCTIONS

1 Preheat the oven to 350°F (180°C, or gas mark 4). Line 9 muffin cups with paper liners.

2 For the graham cracker crust, in a bowl, combine the ground-up crackers with the butter and sugar. (A) Divide the mixture evenly among the muffin cups, adding about 2 heaping table-spoons (25 g) per muffin cup. Press the mixture firmly into the cup until it is ⅛ inch (3 mm) thick. (B) It's okay if some of the crust comes up the sides. Bake the crusts for 10 minutes, rotating and checking the crusts after 5 minutes. Allow to cool completely.

**B**

### If Using Homemade Graham Crackers

The crust should be slightly darker around the edges, with an amber color in the middle, but not dark brown. Notice the color of the crackers before you put the crusts in the oven. As doneness may vary, you may want to reduce the cooking time so that you do not burn the crust.

Press the crust into the cups.

### for smaller hands

Have children mix the crust and press into the cups. Make sure the thickness of the crust is even and firmly packed into the bottom of the muffin cups. ~

**3** Reduce the oven temperature to 325°F (170°C, or gas mark 3). For the cheesecake filling, whip the cream cheese until it is light and fluffy, first with a wooden spoon (C) and then with a whisk. Add the sugar and mix thoroughly. Add the egg, vanilla, lemon zest, and cream and stir until the entire mixture is light and fluffy, scraping down the sides of the bowl with a rubber scraper as needed.

*Mix together the cheesecake filling.*

**C**

4 Distribute the filling evenly among the 9 muffin cups, (D) filling each about halfway. (See page 23 for tips on how to fill muffin cups using the two-spoon method.) Place a roasting pan on the bottom rack of your oven. Place the muffin tin on the middle rack of your oven. Using a teakettle or any pitcher with a pour spout, fill the roasting pan halfway with water.

5 Bake for about 15 minutes, or until the centers are just set. Allow the cheesecakes to cool, then cover with plastic wrap and chill in the fridge for about 2 hours. When ready to serve, remove the plastic wrap, gently peel off the muffin liners, and top with the optional suggested toppings. (Turn off the oven and allow baking pan filled with water to completely cool before removing it.)

**for smaller hands**

Have children watch from a safe distance for steps 4 and 5, especially when you are opening and closing the oven door. ～

*Spoon the cheesecake batter into the cups.*

# Chapter 7

# PARTY FAVORITES
## How to Throw a Fun Cooking-Themed Party

### recipe box

#### COOKIE BAKING PARTY
Peanut Butter and Jelly
Thumbprint Cookies
Chocolate Chip Cookies
Snickerdoodles

#### PIZZA PARTY
Pizza Dough
From-Scratch Tomato Sauce
Personal Pizzas

#### CUPCAKE PARTY
Vanilla Cupcakes
Simple Buttercream Frosting
Cupcake Decorating

# HAPPY BIRTHDAY TO YOU!

Cooking-themed birthday parties are hands-on and fun, and the kids make the food that they eat at the party! The recipes for the parties in this chapter are scaled back so that the yield is smaller. The tricky thing about cooking with a group of kids is that you want to make sure everyone has something to do, but you don't want to end up with more food than your group can eat. Feel free to adjust the amounts if you are looking to feed a large crowd with the food created by the kids.

# TIPS FOR HOSTING A COOKING PARTY

## • Keep the Guest Count Fewer Than Ten

If you would like to invite more guests, plan on working in groups of fewer than ten and have another parent coordinating an activity in another room or outside while you work with one group at a time in the kitchen. For your first cooking birthday party, try a small group of four to six. Large parties in the kitchen can be stressful for a parent who isn't used to cooking with groups of children. Remember, it should be fun for everyone, including you!

## • Be Prepared!

Place all necessary ingredients and tools out and in an area that is not in the way.

## • Children Work Well in Pairs

The recipes in this chapter have a smaller yield so that pairs of kids work on a recipe together. Unless you are looking to have the guests bring home leftovers, have kids make just the right amount for themselves and their parents to sample.

## • Allergies and Dietary Restrictions

Make sure that you are aware of any allergies or dietary restrictions ahead of time.

## • Get Some Help!

Have a parent or two help out during the party. A good ratio of kids to parents is four to one.

## • Make Up Games and Songs

When there is a step that is repetitive and takes a long time, make a game out of it. For example, whipping eggs can be turned into a lively competition and making a song about kneading can pass the time. Kids get burnt out from a task quickly, and I have found that this tactic makes it a lot more fun.

## • Have Parents Bring Extra Bowls and Spoons

Most families do not have five to eight mixing bowls in their home kitchen. Ask guests to bring a mixing bowl and spoon.

## Cookie Recipes

Peanut Butter and Jelly
Thumbprint Cookies

Chocolate Chip Cookies

Snickerdoodles

## Optimal Party Size

4 to 6 kids, ages 8 and up

## Game Plan

2 or 3 work on each item

Each team makes a batch
of cookies, either the
same or different

## A Cookie for Everyone:
# COOKING BAKING PARTY

I have not met a kid who doesn't like making cookies, so a cookie
party is sure to be a blast for everyone.

Yield: **5–7** cookies per person

Here are recipes for three types of cookies that are not only fun to make but also delicious to eat! For this party, I recommend having one parent work with six kids to make the same batch of cookies or having one parent work with each pair of children if you would like to make more than one cookie recipe.

## tips for cookie parties

- Make sure your ingredients are at room temperature. Pull out your butter and eggs an hour before the party starts. Room temperature ingredients are easier to mix. In a pinch, you can microwave butter on a low power setting until it is soft, and you can place eggs in a bowl covered in hot water for 10 minutes to bring them to room temperature quickly.

- Either guide all the groups through the process of making the same cookie or, if you'd like to make all three cookie recipes, have an adult help each team.

- Have multiple containers of ingredients. For example, put flour in a few bowls so that teams can measure at the same time instead of waiting.

- No licking the spoon! Some families allow their kids to eat cookie dough, while others do not. To be on the safe side, do not allow the children to eat raw cookie dough at the party. In the classes I teach I tell kids that we don't eat raw eggs during cooking class, but they can at home with their parents.

- While the cookies are baking, have an activity planned or have the kids play outside once they have helped with the cleanup.

- Have an adult work with the peanut butter cookie team, as the dough is very sticky and the children will need some help forming it into cookies. Rolling the dough in sugar helps with the sticky factor.

- Have copies of the recipes on hand for each team to reference.

- Allow the children to have one cookie at the party and to take the rest home.

## ingredients

- ~ ½ cup (60 g) white whole wheat flour
- ~ ½ cup (60 g) all-purpose flour
- ~ ½ teaspoon baking soda
- ~ 2 teaspoons salt
- ~ 1¼ sticks (10 tablespoons, or 140 g) unsalted butter, at room temperature
- ~ ½ cup (115 g) brown sugar
- ~ ½ cup (100 g) granulated sugar, plus ½ cup (100 g) more for rolling
- ~ 1 large egg
- ~ ¾ cup (195 g) natural creamy peanut butter
- ~ 1 teaspoon pure vanilla extract
- ~ ⅓ cup (85 g) of your family's favorite jam

# *Peanut Butter and Jelly*
# THUMBPRINT COOKIES

These feature the classic PB&J flavors in cookie form. Feel free to swap almond butter in place of the peanut butter. Be sure not to overbake these cookies, as they lose their delightful chewiness when baked until crispy.

Yield: **15** cookies

## tools needed

~ measuring cups and spoons
~ large bowl
~ medium bowl
~ baking sheets
~ parchment paper
~ whisk
~ wooden spoon
~ 2 spoons

# INSTRUCTIONS

1  Preheat the oven to 350°F
   (180°C, or gas mark 4),
   and line baking sheets with
   parchment paper.

2  In a medium bowl, whisk
   together the flours, baking
   soda, and salt. (A)

### for smaller hands

Measuring the dry ingredients
is very fun for small children,
and you'll be surprised by how
seriously they take it, especially
if you show them the proper
way to do it (see page 20). ~

A

Whisk
together dry
ingredients.

*Cream together the butter and sugar.*

## for smaller hands

Have children use a wooden spoon to smash the butter against the sides of the bowl, softening the butter. Then show them how to move the spoon back and forth across the butter to soften it more. Once it is easier to mix, have them switch to a whisk to work more air into the butter. Have teams take turns to avoid tired arms. Or challenge them to use their "big muscles!"  ∼

**5** Because this dough is very sticky, it works best to roll the balls of dough in sugar so that when you make a thumbprint, the dough will not stick to your thumb. Fill a small bowl with the remaining ½ cup (100 g) granulated sugar, and, using the two-spoon measuring technique (see page 23), scoop and drop the cookie dough into the sugar. (C) Toss the cookie dough around to coat before placing it on the prepared baking sheet, leaving about 2 inches (5 cm) of space between cookies. Using your thumb, make a ½-inch (1.3 cm) indentation in the middle of the cookie (D) and fill the thumbprint with about 1 teaspoon jam. (E)

## for smaller hands

Measure out ¼ cup (60 g) of the dough as an example to guide the children with their measurements. Because this dough is very sticky, you may want to toss the dough in the sugar and place it on the baking sheet for them. Handle the dough as if it's a hot potato, just barely touching it with your hands.  ∼

**3** In a large bowl, whip the butter with a wooden spoon until it is smooth and shiny. (B) Gradually add the brown sugar and ½ cup (100 g) granulated sugar until light and fluffy, scraping down the sides of the bowl as needed. Add the egg and mix thoroughly. Add the peanut butter and vanilla, and mix to blend.

**4** Add the dry ingredients in 2 batches, mixing each until just incorporated. Avoid overmixing the dough by having children stop as soon as they can no longer see bits of flour.

*Roll the cookie dough into balls.*

*Using your thumb, make a print in the center of the ball. You may need to make two prints so that it is about the size of a nickel.*

**C**

**D**

Spoon the jam into the thumbprint.

**E**

6 Bake for 12 to 15 minutes, or until the cookies are puffed and slightly golden around the edges but the area around the jam remains pale. Transfer the baking sheets to a rack, and cool the cookies completely on the sheets. They will firm up as they cool.

## ingredients

- ~ 1 cup (120 g) white whole wheat flour
- ~ ¾ cup (90 g) 00 flour, bread flour, or all-purpose flour
- ~ 1 heaping teaspoon baking soda
- ~ ¾ teaspoon baking powder
- ~ ¾ teaspoon salt
- ~ 1¼ sticks (10 tablespoons, or 140 g) unsalted butter, softened
- ~ ¾ cup (170 g) light brown sugar
- ~ ½ cup (100 g) granulated sugar
- ~ 1 large egg
- ~ 1 teaspoon pure vanilla extract
- ~ 2 cups (350 g) semisweet chocolate chips

# CHOCOLATE CHIP COOKIES

These classic chocolate chip cookies are crispy on the outside and slightly chewy on the inside. The addition of bread flour or 00 flour contributes to the chewiness but is not essential to the cookie. These are best served with a cold glass of milk, of course.

*Yield:* 15 *cookies*

## tools needed

~ measuring cups and spoons
~ large mixing bowl
~ medium mixing bowl
~ 2 baking sheets
~ parchment paper
~ whisk
~ wooden spoon
~ rubber spatula
~ 2 spoons

# INSTRUCTIONS

1 Preheat the oven to 350°F (180°C, or gas mark 4) and line baking sheets with parchment paper.

2 In a medium mixing bowl, whisk together the flours, baking soda, baking powder, and salt. Set aside.

### for smaller hands

Have children help measure the ingredients, using the proper measuring technique on page 20. ~

3 Using a wooden spoon, cream the butter and sugars together in a large bowl until smooth, then switch to a whisk to whip until light and fluffy. (See the description of creaming technique on page 23.) Add the egg (A) and vanilla, mixing thoroughly. Scrape down the sides of the bowl with a rubber spatula as needed. (B)

A

*Crack the eggs and add to the dough.*

B

Scrape down the sides of the bowl now and then.

### for smaller hands

Have the children pour in the flour and mix, but tell them to be careful not to overmix the dough. A good rule of thumb is to stop mixing when you can no longer see any bits of flour in the batter.  ~

4 Add the dry ingredients in 2 batches, mixing each time until just combined. Sprinkle in the chocolate chips, and mix to incorporate evenly.

5 Using the two-spoon method (see page 23), form ¼-cup (60 g) pieces of dough into balls and place on the prepared baking sheets. (C) About 6 or 7 scoops of dough fit perfectly on each sheet, allowing plenty of room for the cookies to spread. Bake for 15 to 20 minutes, (D) or until golden brown but still soft.

*Use the two-spoon technique to form the dough into cookies.*

D

Allow cookies
to cool before
serving.

6 Transfer the baking sheets to a
cooling rack for 10 minutes, then
use a spatula to move the cookies
directly onto the rack to cool a
bit longer. These cookies will fall
apart easily if they are moved
before they've had a chance to
cool completely.

PARTY FAVORITES

131

## ingredients

- ~ 1 cup (120 g) all-purpose flour
- ~ ½ cup (60 g) white whole wheat flour
- ~ 1 teaspoon cream of tartar
- ~ ½ teaspoon baking soda
- ~ 1 big pinch salt
- ~ 1 stick (½ cup, or 112 g) unsalted butter, softened
- ~ ¾ cup (150 g) sugar
- ~ 1 large egg

**For Cinnamon Sugar Coating:**
- ~ 2 tablespoons (24 g) sugar
- ~ 1 tablespoon (7 g) ground cinnamon

# SNICKERDOODLES

When we were growing up, these were my sister's favorite cookies.

*Yield:* 15 *cookies*

## tools needed

~ measuring cups and spoons
~ large mixing bowl
~ medium mixing bowl
~ small mixing bowl
~ 2 baking sheets
~ parchment paper
~ whisk
~ wooden spoon
~ rubber spatula
~ 2 spoons

Although I preferred cookies with chocolate chips in them, I always really enjoyed making snickerdoodles with my mom and sister because you roll the cookie dough into balls and toss them in a fragrant mixture of cinnamon and sugar. These cookies will not get brown in the oven, so do not wait for them to do so! They are supposed to be a soft and chewy cookie, thanks to the addition of cream of tartar.

*Measure the dry ingredients.*

# INSTRUCTIONS

**1** Preheat the oven to 400°F (200°C, or gas mark 6) and line baking sheets with parchment paper.

**2** In a medium bowl, whisk together the flours, cream of tartar, baking soda, and salt. Set aside.

**3** In a large mixing bowl, mix the butter with a wooden spoon until it is smooth and shiny. Gradually add the sugar, creaming until light and fluffy. Scrape down the sides of the bowl. Add the egg, and mix thoroughly. Add the dry ingredients in 2 batches, gently mixing after each addition.

### for smaller hands

Using a wooden spoon, smash the butter against the sides of the bowl to soften and loosen the butter. You can also microwave the butter for about 15 seconds to help speed the process. ~

**A**

**B**

Roll the balls in cinnamon sugar.

*Roll the cookie dough into balls.*

4 For the cinnamon sugar topping, in a small bowl, mix together the sugar and cinnamon.

5 Using the two-spoon method (see page 23), form ¼-cup (60 g) portions of dough into balls. (A) Roll the dough balls around in the cinnamon sugar to coat. (B) Place each ball about 2 inches (5 cm) apart on the prepared baking sheets.

### for smaller hands

Have children take turns forming the dough into balls and rolling the balls around in the sugar.  ~

6 Bake for about 10 minutes, or until the cookies are set in the center and begin to crack, rotating the baking sheets after 5 minutes. Note that these cookies will not brown. Transfer the sheets to a wire rack to cool for about 10 minutes before moving the cookies to the rack.

**Optimal Party Size**
6 to 10 kids

**Game Plan**
Each pair of children makes
a batch of pizza dough
*(this makes 2 personal-size pizzas)*

4 to 6 kids make a batch
of tomato sauce
*(this is enough for 5 to 8 pizzas)*

Remaining children prepare
toppings, including grating
cheese and chopping veggies

All children assemble and top
their own pizza

# PIZZA PARTY

Pizza at birthday parties is nothing new, but serving pizza that the kids make themselves is rather unique. A make-your-own pizza party accommodates even picky eaters, allowing kids to decide which toppings they want on their pizzas. And, because you are making the pizza from scratch, you do not have to make traditional round pizzas. Create fun shapes like triangles, hearts, and squares to mix it up and think outside the pizza box.

*Yield:* **1** *pizza per person*

## ingredients

~ ⅓ cup (80 ml) warm water
~ 1 heaping teaspoon active dry yeast
~ ¾ cup (90 g) 00 flour or all-purpose flour
~ ¼ cup (30 g) white whole wheat flour
~ ¼ teaspoon salt
~ 1 tablespoon (15 ml) olive oil, plus more for coating bowl
~ extra flour or semolina for sprinkling

## tools needed
## for each pair of kids

~ measuring cups and spoons
~ liquid measuring cup
~ large mixing bowl
~ medium mixing bowl
~ wooden spoon
~ plastic wrap or large plate

# PIZZA DOUGH

This pizza dough comes together quickly and doesn't need too much time to proof, creating a crust that is soft on the inside and has a crunch on the outside. For a more developed flavor and chewy texture, you can choose a slower proofing method by placing it in the fridge overnight. If you would like to try this method, place the dough in the fridge after step 6 and allow it to proof slowly overnight, covered, or for at least 6 hours.

*Yield:* **2** *personal-size pizza crusts*

# INSTRUCTIONS

1 Measure the water in the liquid measuring cup and sprinkle in the yeast. (A) This activates the yeast.

### for smaller hands

To determine proper water temperature for activating yeast, have children stick a finger in the water. It should feel like a nice warm bath. ~

2 In a large bowl, whisk together the flours and salt. Make a well in the center of the flour.

### for smaller hands

To create a well in the flour, make a fist with your hand. Take your fist and put it in the center of the flour and move it around slightly to make a small circle. You should be able to see the bottom of the bowl. ~

*Activate the yeast in warm water.*

Add the yeast mixture to the flour.

## Mix Slowly!

Before the children begin mixing, show them how to mix slowly, or else they will knock flour out of the bowl and there will be less pizza for them to eat!

*Knead the dough so that it gets stretchy.*

**D**

Before proofing.

After proofing. It's like magic!

### Time-Saving Tip:

A trick to speed the proofing process is to make an at-home proofing box. Turn on your oven to the lowest setting. Once it reaches temperature, turn off the oven and place the dough in the bowls inside. This should shave off about a half hour of proofing time!

3 Once the yeast is foamy, add the olive oil and gently mix. Add the yeast mixture to the well of the flour mixture and mix slowly with a wooden spoon. (B) Once the mixture forms into a shaggy ball and it becomes hard to mix with a spoon, scrape the dough onto a well-floured counter.

4 Knead the dough for 5 to 10 minutes to develop the gluten. (C) See page 25 for a description of how to knead.

5 Clean the bowl and coat the inside of it with a small amount of olive oil. Place the kneaded dough inside the bowl and turn it over to coat with a thin film of oil. (D)

6 Cover the bowl with plastic wrap or a plate that covers the top of the bowl and set aside in a warm place to proof for 1 hour, or until it doubles in size.

PARTY FAVORITES

139

## ingredients

- ~ 1 (13-ounce, or 364 g) can whole peeled tomatoes, drained
- ~ 1 or 2 cloves garlic, peeled
- ~ 2 springs basil
- ~ 2 teaspoons extra-virgin olive oil
- ~ ½ teaspoon vinegar or lemon juice
- ~ salt and pepper to taste

## tools needed

- ~ measuring spoons
- ~ large bowl
- ~ 2 to 5 small bowls
- ~ can opener
- ~ Microplane grater
- ~ citrus juicer, if using lemon instead of vinegar
- ~ wooden spoon

# From-Scratch TOMATO SAUCE

This sauce is bright and fresh, and it is fun for kids to squish the tomatoes with their hands. If there are 10 kids attending the party, have two teams of 2 to 4 kids make batches of this sauce.

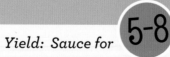

Yield: Sauce for 5-8 personal-size pizzas

**Making the tomato sauce involves four jobs. Choose one or two children to help with each job.**

# INSTRUCTIONS

*Tear the basil gently into pieces.*

1 **Squishing tomatoes:** Give the children a large bowl and the drained tomatoes. Show them how to squish the tomatoes, keeping the tomatoes in the bottom of the bowl to prevent the tomato juice from squirting all over the place.

2 **Grating garlic:** Choose the oldest children for this job. Garlic cloves are small, so it is important that the children are very careful when grating them. Advise them to grate slowly. The garlic will not fall off the Microplane, but rather stick to the underside of it.

3 **Tearing basil:** Choose a few children to tear basil. Have them remove the leaves from the sprig and use their fingertips to gently tear the leaves into pieces that are slightly larger than peas. Explain that it's important to tear rather than crush and rip, because crushing and ripping will cause the basil to turn black.

4 **Mix it all together:** Combine all the prepared ingredients in the bowl with the tomatoes and mix with a wooden spoon. Canned tomatoes may be acidic and seasoned enough that you may not need to add any extra seasonings. Allow the flavors to meld for an hour before adding the sauce to the pizzas.

*Grate the garlic using a Microplane so that it mixes easily into the tomatoes.*

## ingredients

~ Pizza Dough (page 136)
~ flour or semolina
~ From-Scratch Tomato Sauce
  (page 140)

**For Pizza Toppings:**
~ shredded mozzarella cheese
~ sliced mushrooms
~ chopped and sautéed onions
~ fresh basil
~ sliced red bell pepper
~ pepperoni
~ sausage crumbles
~ sliced black olives
~ feta cheese crumbles
~ sliced artichoke hearts

# PERSONAL PIZZAS

Now for the fun part—assembling the pizzas! Most kids just want cheese pizza, but for the more adventurous, have an assortment of veggies and meats on plates that the kids can easily reach. Have some extra dough on hand so that you can demonstrate the following steps before they dive in.

*Yield:* **1** *pizza per person*

## tools needed

~ 2 pizza stones or baking sheets
~ spoon for saucing
~ pizza peels or rimless baking sheets
~ large cutting board
~ pizza cutter

*Sprinkle your work surface with flour or semolina.*

# INSTRUCTIONS

1 About 30 minutes before you are going to bake your pizzas, place pizza stones or upside-down baking sheets in the oven and preheat it to 500°F (250°C, or gas mark 10).

2 Give each pair of children half of their dough recipe. Sprinkle the work surface with flour or semolina (A) and flatten a piece of dough the size of a golf ball with your hands. Make sure the dough doesn't stick to your work surface, sprinkling more flour or semolina under the pizza dough as needed. Flatten the dough with your hands until it is consistently ½ inch (1.3 cm) thick, both on the edges and in the middle. Each pizza should be 6 to 7 inches (15 to 17.5 cm) in diameter. (B)

Using your hands, flatten out the dough.

(C)

*Before adding sauces and toppings,
make sure your pizza can move around.*

3 Before adding the sauce and toppings to the pizza, try the "Wiggle Test"—slide the rolled-out dough around a little bit to make sure it isn't sticking to your work surface. (C) If it is, sprinkle more flour or semolina underneath!

4 Add 1 to 2 tablespoons (15 to 30 ml) of sauce to your pizza with a spoon, leaving a border for the crust. Sprinkle on the cheese (not too much!).

5 Sprinkle a few toppings on the pizza, but do so sparingly—this type of pizza dough isn't meant to be overloaded with toppings. Cheese goes on first, then any additional toppings.

Toppings ready for pizzas!

*...uce your pizza with a spoon, leaving ...border around the edge for the crust.*

*Sprinkle the cheese on first.*

*Add toppings sparingly.*

6 Make sure that only adults transfer the pizzas to the hot oven. Use a pizza peel or rimless baking sheet to lift the pizzas off the counter. Sprinkle a small amount of semolina on the pizza peel to help the pizza slide off. To place in the oven, carefully slide the baking sheet or pizza peel over the hot stone (or baking sheet) and in a swift motion, jerk forward and immediately backward to release and slide the pizza onto the stone. This may take a little practice, so be sure to try it before the party! If you do not feel comfortable with this technique, you can also bake pizzas directly on baking sheets placed on top of the preheated baking sheets in the oven.

7 Bake the pizzas for 5 to 10 minutes, and watch carefully to make sure they don't overbake. The pizzas are done when they are golden brown on the bottom center.

8 Remove the pizzas from the oven by sliding a pizza peel or rimless baking sheet under the crust and lifting the pizza out of the oven. Slide the pizza onto a large cutting board, allow to cool for a few minutes, then slice and eat!

Make name tags attached to toothpicks so you know whose pizza is whose. To make mini name tags, you'll need toothpicks, masking tape, and a permanent marker. Take a 1- to 2-inch (2.5 to 5 cm) piece of masking tape and fold it on the toothpick to seal the sticky sides together. With a permanent marker, write the names of children on the tape. Toothpicks can be inserted into the crusts of the pizza after baking. Create a map of the pizzas in the oven to help you remember whose pizza is whose.

## Optimal Party Size
6 to 9 kids

## Game Plan
2 or 3 children work on a team

Each team makes 6 cupcakes
*(2 or 3 cupcakes per person)*

Each team makes a batch
of frosting
*(enough to frost 6 cupcakes)*

Children decorate their own
cupcakes

# CUPCAKE PARTY

**Cupcakes are fun, delicious, and festive. Having children decorate their own cupcakes provides a creative outlet, allowing them to turn their cupcake into a work of art.**

*Yield:* **2-3** *cupcakes per person*

## ingredients

- ¾ cup (90 g) cake flour
- 1 teaspoon baking powder
- pinch of salt
- ½ stick (4 tablespoons, or 56 g) unsalted butter, softened
- ½ cup (100 g) sugar
- ¼ teaspoon pure vanilla extract
- 1 large egg, at room temperature
- ¼ cup (60 ml) milk, at room temperature

## tools needed

- measuring cups and spoons
- liquid measuring cup
- 2 large mixing bowls
- medium mixing bowl
- standard-size 12-cup muffin tin
- muffin liners
- whisk
- wooden spoon or spatula

# VANILLA CUPCAKES

**After many recipe tests with various flours, cake flour made the fluffiest and most tender cake.**

*Yield:* **6** *cupcakes*

If you do not have cake flour on hand and do not want to go to the store to get it, you can use pastry flour instead, but you'll need to add a few minutes to the baking time. I do *not* recommend all-purpose flour for this recipe, because the resulting cake will be too dense. I suggest using granulated white sugar instead of natural cane sugar. It's very important to use room temperature butter, eggs, and milk when making this recipe.

## Why Such a Small Yield?

Having a group of 2 or 3 children make a batch of 6 cupcakes is the perfect amount to ensure that kids and parents each get a cupcake at the end of the party. The cupcake recipe here can easily be doubled or quadrupled. In fact, the recipe is based on a traditional 1-2-3-4 ratio cake, which stands for 1 cup each (225 g) butter and (235 ml) milk, 2 cups (400 g) sugar, 3 cups (360 g) self-rising flour (we are using cake flour with baking powder added as a leavener), and 4 eggs.

*Gradually add the sugar to the butter.*

A

# INSTRUCTIONS

1 Preheat the oven to 350°F (180°C, or gas mark 4). Have children place muffin liners in the tins, making sure they take time to separate the papers.

2 In a medium bowl, whisk together the flour, baking powder, and salt. Set aside.

3 In a large mixing bowl, beat the butter until it is smooth and shiny. Gradually add the sugar in 2 batches. (A) Continue to beat for 2 to 3 minutes, until the mixture is light and fluffy. Don't skimp on this part! Add the vanilla and mix to combine.

## for smaller hands

Using a wooden spoon, smash the butter against the sides of the bowl to soften and loosen it. Then move the spoon back and forth across the butter to further soften it. Once it is easier to mix, switch to a whisk to incorporate more air into the butter. Have children take turns to avoid tired arms. Or challenge them to use their "big muscles!" ~

*Add the egg yolk to the butter mixture.*

## for smaller hands

To avoid having the kids get burnt out on whipping the whites, turn the egg white whisking into a competition! Make sure that both teams start at the same time and see who finishes first. The winner is the first team to obtain stiff peaks, meaning that when they lift up the whisk, the egg white forms a point. ~

4 Separate the egg for the children, placing the yolk in the butter and sugar mixture (B) and the white in a separate large bowl. Whisk the egg yolk into the butter and sugar mixture until it turns to a pale yellow fluffy consistency.

## for smaller hands

Trust me on this one: You'll want to separate the egg for young children. If any egg yolk gets into the whites, it makes it really difficult to whip to stiff peaks. Make sure that the kids start mixing slowly once you add the egg yolk to avoid slopping the egg out of the bowl. Once the egg yolk is mostly combined, they can go to town on whisking it up. ~

5 Alternate adding the flour mixture and the milk, (C, D) starting and ending with one-third of the flour mixture. Mix in each addition until just incorporated. Be careful not to overmix.

6 Meanwhile, whisk the egg white until it reaches stiff peaks. Mix one-third of the egg white into the batter, and then gently fold in the rest until it is just incorporated. (See the folding technique on page 25 for more details about this step.)

7 With two spoons, fill the lined muffin cups about three-fourths of the way up. Use one spoon to scoop and the second spoon to scrape the batter into the cups. (See the two-spoon method on page 23 for more details about this step.)

*Alternate adding the flour and milk, starting and ending with the flour.*

*Add half the milk after the first third of the flour.*

### for smaller hands

Fill one muffin tin in each team's pan as an example of how much batter should be in each cup. Most kids naturally want to fill it all the way up to the top! ~

### Chocolate Cupcakes Variation

To make chocolate cupcakes, add ¼ cup (30 g) cocoa powder to the flour mixture and proceed with the recipe.

8 Place in the preheated oven and close the door. Do not open the oven door for the first 10 minutes of baking, as this will cause the oven temperature to drop, potentially deflating your cupcakes. Rotate the pans after 10 minutes. Bake for 5 minutes more, or until just set. The cupcakes are finished when a wooden skewer inserted into the center comes out clean. Cool in the pan for 10 minutes, then remove from the pan and cool completely on a rack before frosting. This usually takes 15 to 20 minutes. You can speed the cooling process by popping them in the fridge for 5 minutes once they have cooled in the pan for 10 minutes.

## ingredients

- ~ ½ stick (4 tablespoons, or 56 g) unsalted butter, softened
- ~ ¾ cup (90 g) powdered sugar
- ~ 1 teaspoon milk, as needed
- ~ ¼ teaspoon pure vanilla extract
- ~ pinch of salt

## tools needed

- ~ measuring cups and spoons
- ~ medium mixing bowl
- ~ wooden spoon
- ~ spatula

# *Simple* BUTTERCREAM FROSTING

When I make a simple buttercream frosting, I never use a recipe. That's how my grandma and mom have always made it, too.

*Yield: Enough to frost*  **6** *cupcakes*

By not relying on a recipe, you're free to think for yourself, which ultimately makes you a better cook. I recommend making this base recipe a few times to get the hang of it before trying it without the recipe. This is a very intuitive frosting, and you can easily taste and adjust the amounts as needed. Kids love being the designated taste testers!

### for smaller hands

Show children how to stir slowly to avoid tossing powdered sugar into the air. ~

# INSTRUCTIONS

1   In a medium mixing bowl, beat the butter with a wooden spoon until it is smooth and shiny.

2   Gradually add the sugar in ¼-cup (30 g) increments. Avoid the temptation to add the sugar all at once; it is a lot easier to mix in smaller amounts. Feel free to add a small amount of milk if the mixture seems too dry.

3   Add the vanilla (or other flavorings; see page 154) and a pinch of salt and continue to mix until it becomes light and fluffy, adding milk if needed to achieve spreading consistency.

*Add jam to buttercream for flavor and color.*

*Add cocoa powder to buttercream to make chocolate frosting.*

## for smaller hands

If each of the children wants to make a different frosting, have them make the base recipe, then place a small amount in a bowl so that they can add flavors individually. You'll want to decrease the amounts in the flavor recipes here to adjust for the amount of frosting that is in the bowl. ~

For lemon frosting, add lemon zest.

## Natural Frosting Flavor Variations

Although adding food coloring is fun, it isn't the most natural option. Take a look at some ideas for natural frostings that add color *and* flavor.

### Cherry Frosting

Add a spoonful of cherry preserves and garnish with a natural maraschino cherry or fresh cherry. Feel free to add your favorite jam, or make your own fresh cherry preserves. Simply heat 1½ cups (225 g) fresh or frozen cherries with 1 tablespoon (12 g) sugar in a medium saucepan and simmer over low heat for 20 to 30 minutes, stirring often. Remove from the heat and allow to cool before pureeing.

### Chocolate Frosting

Add 1 tablespoon (8 g) cocoa powder to the mixture. You may need to add a splash of milk to compensate for the cocoa. Garnish with chocolate shavings.

### Lemon or Orange Frosting

Add the zest of 1 lemon or orange and a squeeze of the juice, adding more as necessary. Reserve some of the zest to garnish the top.

### Mint Frosting

Add a scant ¼ teaspoon peppermint extract and finely chopped peppermint to the mixture. Garnish the cupcake with a mint leaf.

*Add mint extract and chopped fresh mint for mint frosting.*

## ingredients

~ Simple Buttercream Frosting
  (page 152)
~ Vanilla Cupcakes (page 148)
~ decorative garnishes: a rainbow of
  colored sugars, chocolate shavings,
  edible sparkles, and sprinkles

## tools needed

~ frosting piping bags
~ frosting tips in a variety of sizes
~ rubber band
~ offset spatula

# CUPCAKE DECORATING

Now for the moment we've all been waiting for...
it's time to decorate the cupcakes!

*Yield:*  *cupcakes per person*

## How to Use a Piping Bag

Show children how to squeeze from the back, and practice piping the frosting onto a plate before decorating their cupcakes. Frosting used for practicing can be scraped up and placed back into the piping bags. Start from the center of the cupcake and work your way out to the edges, working in a circle. Or simply scoop some frosting from a bowl and, using an offset spatula, spread the frosting to the edges of the cupcake.

1 Cover the table with an oilcloth covering and arrange the bowls of frostings down the center. Once the cupcakes have cooled, ask children which frostings they would like to use, and have the kids sit near the frosting of their choice. Place cupcakes on a napkin or plate in front of each child.

2 To frost cupcakes, place the frosting in piping bags fitted with tips in a variety of sizes. (A) Propping the bag in a bowl or measuring cup, tip side down, spoon the frosting into the piping bag until it is half full. Make sure that the end of the frosting bag is secured with a rubber band to prevent frosting from leaking out the back.

*It is easier to manage a half-full piping bag than one that is completely full.*

3 Fill small dishes with a variety of sprinkles and garnishes and place garnishes down the center of the table. (B) Don't put out all the sprinkles just in case one child from a team uses up all of their sprinkles before the other teammate has a chance to garnish.

*Using a star-tipped piping bag, make fun borders on your cupcakes.*

Sprinkles are fun for all ages.

# ABOUT THE AUTHOR

**Leah Brooks began her culinary career in the beautiful Pacific Northwest, where she grew up.**

She graduated from the Art Institute of Seattle's culinary program and worked under two of Seattle's James Beard Award–winning chefs for seven years. Leah currently lives in the San Francisco Bay Area, where she shares her passion for local fresh foods with young people in her celebrated hands-on cooking classes at Young Urban Modern Chefs (Y.U.M. Chefs). Leah's work has been featured in the *Wall Street Journal* as well as on local Bay Area parent resource websites.

# ACKNOWLEDGMENTS

**For all the help I received putting this book together, I would like to thank the following people:**

All the kids who have come into my kitchen eager to learn and eat delicious food! Your smiles and enthusiasm inspire me each and every day. A very special thanks to Georgia B., Josie F., Shikha J., Vihaan U., Lindsay L., Isabell M., Madison W., Visarutha W., Mason V., Molly and Leslie C., Erroll and Audrey C., Zara P., Lola and Nina A., Valentino V.G., Olivia G., Paige P.D., Mason and William S.D., and Sage and Simone J.B. for being the best little chefs in the photo shoots!

My supportive husband, Dana, for being a dutiful taste tester and my rock.

My mom, for always believing in me; my sister, for always appreciating the food I make; and my dad, for always being proud of me.

My recipe testers—Ginny, Shannon, Mom, and Katie— thank you for taking time out of your busy schedules to bake for me!

The talented photographer Scott Peterson, who captured the food the kids and I created in such a beautiful way. To Carolyn Edgecomb and Wei Han Tseng, who helped out so very much during the photo shoots!

Open Mind and the Katherine Michiels School, for providing a beautiful kitchen in which to shoot the photos and an inspiring place to share my craft.

And a special thanks to Quarry Books, for giving me the opportunity to share my love of baking and cooking with kids with a wider audience.

# ALSO AVAILABLE:

### Gardening Lab for Kids,
978-1-58923-904-8

### Music Lab: We Rock!,
978-1-59253-921-5

### Kitchen Science Lab for Kids,
978-1-59253-925-3

### Noodle Kids,
978-1-59253-963-5